God's Transforming Love

God's Transforming Love

Faith, Restoration, and Purpose

PRESENTED BY LILLY LESTER

God's Transforming Love © 2016 by Lilly Lester

All rights reserved, except for brief quotations used in review, articles or other forms of media. No part of this book may be reproduced or transmitted in any form or by any means, electronically or mechanically, including photocopying, recording or by information storage or retrieval systems without permission from the publisher.

Scripture quotations marked KJV are taken from the King James Version. Public domain.

Scripture quotations marked NKJV are taken from the New King James Version ® Bible ©1982 by Thomas Nelson, Inc. Used with permission. All rights reserved.

Scripture quotations marked HCSB have been taken from the Holman Christian Standard Bible®. Copyright © 1999, 2000, 2002, 2003, 2009 by Holman Bible Publishers. Used by permission. HCSB® is a federally registered trademark of Holman Bible Publishers.

Scripture quotations marked NCV are taken from the New Century Version®. © 2005 by Thomas Nelson. Used by permission. All rights reserved.

Scripture quotations marked NIV are taken the Holy Bible, New International Version®, NIV®. Copyright © 1973, 1978, 1984, 2011 by Biblica, Inc.® Used by permission of Zondervan. All rights reserved worldwide. www.zondervan.com. The "NIV" and "New International Version" are trademarks registered in the United States Patent and Trademark Office by Biblica, Inc.®

Scripture quotations marked AMP are taken from the Amplified® Bible. Copyright © 1954, 1958, 1962, 1964, 1965, 1987 by The Lockman Foundation. Used by permission. (www.Lockman.org)

ISBN 978-1-944440-01-5

Printed in the United States of America

Table of Contents

Foreword 7

Introduction 9
Lilly Lester

A Prophetic Tribute to All Women 11
Lilly Lester

How to Glean From This Book 12
Karynthia A. G. Phillips

Section I: Faith Is a Journey 15

Faith Reflection 16
Lilly Lester

To Teach Me 18
Patricia Kluttz

A Simplistic Faith 27
Ariel Jones

Just When I Thought This Chapter Was Closed 31
Regina Conley-Hockett

Until Death Do Us Part 35
Gwendolyn E. Mackey-Google

Transformation by Multiple Transitions 44
Rev. Lalita R. Smith

A Blessed Journey 53
Wanda Hodge

Moments of Reflection 58
Lilly Lester

Section II: Restoration 59

Restoration Reflection 60
Lilly Lester

Crossroads to Personal Wholeness 61
Karynthia A.G.Phillips

My Story, His Glory 71
Joy Lester Perez

Trust: It's Just a Journey 75
Dr. Karen Wilkerson

My Secret Shame 85
Courtney Salters

Grace, Kindness, and Pure Love 93
Raquel Gammon

A Contemporary Woman at the Well................ 100
Sonya Little-Jones

Personal Life Reflections 106
By Lilly Lester

Section III: Discovering and Fighting for Purpose... 107

Purpose Reflection.. 108
Lilly Lester

A Chosen Vessel 109
Lucille H. Smith

After the Divorce, Out of the Pit 116
Crystal Martin

Not Forgotten 119
Sherry Jackson

Our Life Speaks 123
Tonia Scott

This Is My Story; This Is My Song 129
Denotra Sneed

Eulogy of an Angel Reacher............................ 133
Marva Southall

Personal Life Reflection 139
Lilly Lester

Epilogue 141
Dr. Peggy Enochs

Contributors 143

Foreword

There are many people serving God; however, they have not connected the relevance in their minds to their present or future situations. Thus one might say, "How could a God of love allow such suffering, trials, and tribulations to plague their lives? Why are not all prosperous and happy? Walking by faith seems so impossible. How does the Bible even apply to me? These are questions and statements that I have observed through my years of pastoral care, community involvement, and just being a human being involved with other people.

In contrast, let us look at women in the past as we review stories in the Bible, which occurred centuries ago and are often considered folklore. These biblical women were women who actually lived on this earth. For example, the woman at the well, who lived a life of promiscuity but met the compassion of Jesus; Ruth, who lost her husband and her only means of financial support; Bathsheba, who committed adultery and became pregnant by her lover (King David, who also had her husband murdered); Tamar, who was raped by her brother; and Abigail, who was married to Nabal, who was described as a fool in the Bible. These happenings from long ago may seem unreal to many readers.

The stories in this book, God's Transforming Love, are by 21st-century women whose lives have been transformed. Their testimonies bring to life the message of the Bible. God loves. God heals. God restores. God gives meaning and purpose to life. But you must receive it by faith, which gives you an overcoming, conquering power to move forward past all of the challenges of life.

Lastly, I believe that the testimonies in this book embody the Scripture verses found in Romans 8:35, 37: "Who shall separate us from the love of Christ? Shall tribulation, or distress, or persecution, or famine, or nakedness, or peril, or sword? … Yet in all these things we are more than conquerors through Him who loved us" (NKJV).

Pastor Angela Roberts Jones

Lilly Lester is a retired Educator and founder of Love Joy Collections and Creative Hands Writing Group. She has been an advocate for women and children for over 30 years. Her passions include spending time with her family, writing, and women's ministry. Lilly has authored four inspirational books and co–authored three others. Her writings and teachings have coached women to ignite and fan the flame into their kingdom purpose and to embrace change with anticipation and gratitude. Lilly is a retreat leader, teacher, speaker, and spiritual midwife that inspires and impacts women from all walks of life. Lilly resides in Nashville, Tennessee with her husband of 49 years. They have two adult children, five grandchildren, and many spiritual sons and daughters.

Introduction

On a frosty winter Saturday morning, a couple of friends and I decided to look in on an estate sale across town. Not looking for anything in particular, I wondered why I was out on this cold winter morning. As we browsed through this beautiful unoccupied home, a large waning plant caught my attention. I called my friends over to look at the once beautiful plant. They were unimpressed and chided me to come along. As I walked throughout the house my mind kept going back to the sick plant. I then turned and rushed back to the plant as if someone else might buy it. As I touched the fragile limbs, I noticed there were only a few leaves at its tips. God's transforming love flooded my thoughts and visions of how He takes care and loves us when we are broken, rejected, and lost.

I asked the attendant the price of the plant, knowing no matter the cost, I had to have it. I transported the plant home, careful not to break the sagging limbs. Just as the plant was moved and settled into a nice lighted area, one of the weaker limbs broke in half. I took the broken piece, with its near withered leaves on the end, and put it in some water; frantically hoping it would not die. After three days, I put the broken end back in the dirt with its family. Three months have passed and I've intentionally loved, cared, and spoken life into this forgotten plant. I saw it literally transform from death to life! Its limbs are upright and the leaves vibrant and green are unfolding daily. How much more will God's love transform us when we intentionally yield ourselves and our wills to Him?

God's Transforming Love recognizes the power and availability of God's love in every state of weakness we may find ourselves. Life will happen. A variation of seasons in our lives can sometimes be overwhelming and leave us fragmented. We look and long for clarity that can only be found in Christ Jesus. Because of his finished work on the cross, all blessings, healings, wealth, and power has been added to our lives. No longer must we walk by sight, accepting a counterfeit love. God's love is one of covenant, faithfulness, mercy, loving kindness, and full of grace. God lovingly waits for us to turn to Him in obedience. It is only then that He changes our condition, nature, and perspective. Spiritual transformation starts in the mind and heart. (Romans 12:2 NKJV) "Do not conform to the pattern of this world, but be transformed by the renewing of your mind. Then you will be able to test and approve what God's will is.... His good, pleasing and perfect will.

God's Transforming Love is written by eighteen remarkable women whose appointed time is "now" to proclaim the power and beauty of God's Transforming Love to the world. These women have faith to believe. They have been restored. They have purpose for living and being. Our prayer for every reader is that you will experience the power and beauty of God's transforming love in your personal life, which He freely gives to those who passionately desire to know Him more intimately.

Lilly Lester

A Prophetic Tribute to ALL Women

The Victor's Crown

Lilly Lester

My Precious Daughters, this is your season!
Stay positioned in Me, that you may reason:
Plans I have purposed just for you:
My grace is sufficient to see you through.
Surrender the old, embrace the new,
You are my chosen; I favor you.
Fear not, it's time to let go and fly:
Your wings are no longer wet, but dry,
Do not hide when strong winds come:
I am your fortress in the storm.
Conquer your ground by speaking My Word!
Bold and powerful wherever heard:
I will place jewels in your crown,
That My glory may be renowned.
You are no longer ordinary you see!
You are now Satan's arch enemy!
My transforming love has made you new,
Whole and holy through and through:
Today you give a brand-new sound,
Because you wear the Victor's Crown.

To bring Vashti the queen before the king with the crown royal, to show the people and the princes her beauty: for she was fair to look on. Esther 1:11 (KJV)

How To Glean From This Book

Karynthia A. G. Phillips

The gem you hold, *God's Transforming Love,* will offer tranquility, wisdom, and empowerment as you read, meditate and pray for God to reveal how you should translate these experiences in your life. Use each story to obtain strength for your journey. Please, let me encourage you not to read through speedily, but patiently. As you read, listen to the voice of each writer. As the Holy Spirit opens your eyes to their hearts, see how they have embraced God's Word to become fashioned into the women designed by the Master Visionary.

This labor of love is one that echoes the heartfelt words of women who have experienced the hand of God as a lump of clay in the hands of a skilled potter. Like a lump of clay, the formation is often pulled, tugged, pinched, and folded as if it worships its Creator amidst the vicissitudes of one's existence. It is with the gifted hands of the Master Craftsman that a transformation occurs, that is so dramatic, it is etched in the walls of one's memory. The disfigurement that life can hand us, as God shapes the destiny and purpose by His transforming love, is revealed in the following pages by the eighteen ladies who have written their story.

God's Transforming Love can be used as a road map on many paths you may travel in life. This book can be used as a Bible study tool, for quiet time meditation, for journaling experiences, during small group discussion, and as a mentoring guide for clarity of transitions. I challenge you to become transformed by God's love as these writers, who have submitted their works.

God's Transforming Love is a book of stories written by eighteen ladies. It is divided into three Sections: Faith, Restoration, and Purpose. Each Section begins with a Reflection that gives you a focal point or overview for each story in that section. Also, a scripture for meditation is provided with this Reflection. The stories then follow. After which, there is a Personal Life Reflection piece at the end of the three Sections. Here, the reader is afforded the opportunity to ponder, meditate and make life application in response to the questions raised.

There are numerous ways one can glean from this book. As well, your own creative juices may add to this process. I submit the follow suggestions:

1. Read as a collection of short stories and testimonies

2. Use as a devotional guide

a. Start reading from the beginning of the book or choose a Section that applies to your season of life or area of interest (i.e., Faith, Restoration, and Purpose). Yes, you may read out of order.

b. Reflect and use the questions listed in Personal Life Reflections to capture the essence of what God is speaking to you.

c. Review the writer's Scripture verse choices and those you sense God is leading you to read and meditate on them.

d. Journal your experience. Write down your thoughts as they flow through your mind, without regard to spelling, grammar, etc. This can help you to clarify direction and hear your inner self.

e. Pray for insight and direction as to how you are to implement the life lessons. There might be occasion when you have to reread a story or particular section. Do not be disappointed! You are not in a competition. Transformation is a process and each transformation requires a different method for completion.

3. Use as a small group Bible Study. You and the members of the group can identify which women of the Bible are comparable with these women of the twenty- first century in this book. Discuss why and how their stories are similar.

Grab a cup of tea and get started on a journey of hope, laughter, and tears arriving at a destination of fulfillment—transformed.

Section 1

Faith Is a Journey

Faith Reflection

Lilly Lester

Christ is not physically present; therefore, believers in Him must walk by faith. Remember what the Bible teaches: "Faith is the substance of things hoped for, the evidence of things not seen" (Hebrews 11:1 NKJV). Let us unpack this action definition of faith by describing what faith does. A substance means "essence" or "reality" of a thing. Faith treats the things hoped for as reality, with evidence or proof of what may not be seen at the time it is spoken. Faith itself cannot be seen or touched. It can be only trusted, relied on, and believed—that's hope.

What is our reaction when life happens and we find ourselves faced with dire circumstances that we never dreamed we would encounter? We will encounter situations that actually put our faith on trial.

Dear hearts, according to 1 Peter 4:12–19 (KJV), you should not be surprised by trials, but you should continue to commit yourself to God and keep doing what is right through every trial. Peter goes on to say that when your faith is tried, it is far more precious than pure gold. Trials also can result in purifying our souls as it strengthens our faith. Just as fire removes the impurities from gold, trials help you recognize the impurities of doubt and unbelief that have become an integral part of our thinking and emotions.

Faith in God removes the dependence on ourselves and our attachments to the world. Faith reminds us that God is sufficient and all powerful. Faith begins where man's power ends. Vance Harner, an author said, *"Nothing is more disastrous than to study faith, analyze faith, make noble resolves of faith, but never actually to make the leap of faith."*

Section 1: Faith Is a Journey

Believing that God is the almighty, all powerful God of impossibility is the first step toward faith. Doubt is the enemy of faith. Why not begin now to feed your faith through God's Word, prayer, and fellowship with other believers? Faith moves mountains; doubts help create mountains. Determine today to starve doubt by refusing to remain the victim. Faith renders the victor's crown. In this section there are seven stories that share walks of faith. Faith that has been tried and tested. Faith that had to have a corresponding action of believing and speaking life. A faith that resolved to walk by faith and not by sight.

"But without faith it is impossible to please Him, for he who comes to God must believe that

He is, and that He is a rewarder of those who diligently seek Him." Hebrew 11:6 (NKJV)

God's Transforming Love

Patricia Kluttz a native Bostonian, currently resides in Nashville, Tennessee, with her four children and six grandchildren. Patricia is a founding teacher in Nashville's first public Montessori school. She attends Born Again Church, where she enjoys being a part of the backstage crew in their Living Parables Ministry. Contrary to popular belief, working out takes a backseat to family and friends. She loves to laugh and hang out with her children. She loves music, the outdoors, and teaching and working with children. Patricia desires to one day go back to school and earn her doctorate in literacy. Patricia published her first book—a children's alphabet book—when a part of the nation of Islam. She is working toward publishing two more children's books. She loves life and God!

To Teach Me

Patricia Kluttz

I can still remember that scorching hot day in July when my life was changed forever. I had promised my children that we would go swimming, and boy, did they let me know how desperately they wanted to go. As we walked to the apartment complex's pool, the normally short walk that day seemed miles away. My children were beyond

Section 1: Faith Is a Journey

excited; they seemed to be getting energized by the heat so much so that I promised them that the next time we would bring Daddy along to join the fun. After a few hours of swimming, we returned home. My husband met us at the door, thankful that he had missed the swimming fun with our four energetic angels. I collapsed across my bed, praying for strength to get up to bathe and feed the kids.

As I lay there recuperating from the fun-filled day we had all enjoyed, the telephone rang. I continued to lay there resting as my husband answered the phone. After a brief exchange of pleasantries, he gave the phone to me and announced that it was my sister, Janice, calling from Hilton Head Island. Life seemed to jump back into my tired, sun-drained body.

"What's up, my sister? How goes the Island?"

"Trie', Trie'!" my sister said, trying to get my attention.

"What's Ma doing? Let me talk to her!" I said, cutting her off.

You see my mother had just spent a few days with me in Nashville and then she went to Hilton Head to visit my sisters who live there.

"Trie', that's why I am calling. It's Ma. She's in a coma!"

I am not sure what happened next. All I remember is being on the floor, gasping for air and crying! Disbelief flooded my mind.

"Oh, my God," I thought.

My stomach and chest felt like someone had repeatedly punched me; they hurt so badly. Somebody helped me understand. I looked at my husband who was asking questions and trying to understand what was being said to me on the other end of the receiver, but I couldn't speak. I was confused. I had just talked with my mother the previous night . . . she just left Nashville a couple of days ago, and we talked about her moving down here and living with me.

Okay, hold on! Wait just one minute; this was Ma she was talking about. I don't remember if I was thinking these things or saying them out loud.

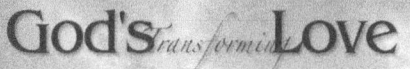

Come on, not my mother, God, please! Please let Janice be joking.

The air seemed to be leaving my body, and I was going numb. I ached deep in my body. It was a pain I had never experienced before or since.

"Trie', Trie! *Patricia*! Are you okay?" Janice asked.

Tears came streaming down my face as the news about my mother started to register. I stared at my husband. I couldn't speak. I couldn't keep standing. I just sank to the floor.

Please, God. Please let this be a joke! "Jan, where's Ma? Let me talk to her!" I demanded. "Janice, please, please put Ma on the phone," was all I could say between the pain, the shock, and the loss of breath.

My husband took the phone out of my hands and I heard him say, "She'll be on the next flight out."

"Ma, I'm on my way. Here I come! Hang in there, it will be all right!"

I knew when I walked into her hospital room and she heard my voice, she would smile and wake up. Yup, she'll be okay. *Hold on, Ma. I am coming!*

By the time I reached the hospital, Ma had died! She passed away . . . Ma was gone!

Fear gripped me, and sadness engulfed me. *Ma, what am I going to do without you? Ma, why you? Why now? I love you and need you! Ma, how am I going to make it? Please, God, bring her back. She's my world, and I'm her baby girl...Now what? Who will I turn to? Who will I be able to depend on?*

I walked around for a very long time just going through the motions. I was sinking deeper and deeper into a pit of depression and didn't realize it. I remembered once when a friend was complaining about her mom and how her mom got on her nerves, and I told her if it were so bad, why not let her mother and my mother change places! I tried not to cry in front of anyone or let my true feelings show, I just

Section I: Faith Is a Journey

wanted to go away and be alone. I didn't think I was going to make it. All I knew was that my mother was no longer with me. My friend, my confidant, my girl was gone.

As time passed, I told myself I had to pull myself together. I had four young children and a husband who needed and loved me, the same way I loved and needed my mom. I put forth an honest effort to get my life back on track; I started working full-time, going to school full-time, and raising my family, but something was wrong. Something was still missing. There was an emptiness, a major void in my life and in my heart. I now realize that when things are out of control in my life, I have a tendency to get real busy. Things were definitely out of control, and so I did what I had always done; got real busy.

Meanwhile, my marriage was slowly deteriorating. When I met my husband, I was a student at Spelman College, and he was a student at Morehouse College. We had a great relationship. We had our issues in the early stages of our relationship, but as we grew up, we grew together. I often describe it as: when he sneezed, I blew my nose; if he got cut, I bled. We meshed like a hand in a glove. He was very caring and attentive as a husband and later as a dad. Then things started to change.

The changes occurred slowly, and they were very subtle. With my husband, a Muslim, and me trying to salvage our marriage, I joined the Nation of Islam. I thought that would help make things better, but it didn't, I couldn't fix it. We eventually lost trust and respect for each other. So, I threw myself into work, school, and the children. At first I didn't realize that those things were taking a toll on the marriage, and then I got to the place where I didn't care anymore. During this time, I began to notice small changes in him. He missed more and more days from work. He stayed out later and later, and he began to drink and stock the refrigerator with beer. He had even begun smoking.

Communicating, at best, was difficult, and we would always end up pointing the finger at each other. Soon money and property began to go missing from the house. When I would ask him about the items that were missing, he would tell me I misplaced them. It took a long time before I realized he was selling our possessions to support his drug habit. I was miserable and furious. I was sad because I knew what a wonderful person he was and the potential he had. I was angry because I felt we had the same struggles, and why did he get to escape them by going into a world of drugs and leave me alone to raise our four children? Again, I found myself left alone by someone I loved and needed. Never in a million years would I have thought I would be a single parent.

"God, what did I do so wrong to be left alone again?" People say there are always red flags, but I didn't see them. Here was a man who didn't as much as smoke, and then he ends up on drugs. I blamed myself for a very long time. *"If only I . . ."* went through my mind. I went through my days with blinders on. I did what I had to do to raise my precious children who didn't ask for any of this and who were counting on me alone.

Between the two losses and living in a city where I had no family, I didn't think I would be able to physically or mentally make it. Then one spring day I was standing on the balcony of my apartment and I began to cry; the heaviness of my life was more than I could bear any longer. I can still see the contrast of colors in the sky as the sun began to set—the vibrant reds, yellows, and oranges against the dark clouds. Even through my tears, I could see God's beauty. There I stood in the mist of God's wondrous work, and all I could come up with was: Why, why me?

I was still trying to make sense of this mess I called my life. I was still trying to figure out how I was going to make it. I prayed, "Help me, God. Help me understand what I need to do. I can't fake it any longer. I'm tired and I'm desperate."

I actually told God I didn't want to live anymore. I don't remember ever feeling as alone as I did at that point. Right then and there I needed direction; I needed help. Although I was raised in the church, loved God, accepted Jesus and believed I was sold out for Christ, I had not

Section 1: Faith Is a Journey

learned how to walk by faith. I never learned how to put all my faith and trust in God. I was at my breaking point.

"God I need someone, something I can depend on, to put my trust in and lean on," I prayed. I needed consistency. Then the Scripture came back to: "Jesus Christ is the same yesterday and today and forever" (Hebrews 13:8 NIV). I grabbed ahold of that Scripture verse and held on to for dear life.

One thing I was certain of was that God was real, and even though I had allowed my concept of who Jesus was to become cloudy, I knew God was the Creator of all things and maybe He could help me. That was the day I decided I would ask God to help me. I still wasn't sure about Jesus, but I knew there was someone greater than me, and I needed His help. My world was rapidly crashing down around me.

So there I was standing on the balcony a few years after the loss of my mother. I was a divorced mother of four children, still working and going to school full-time, and still very lost. I cried out to God, asking—begging—Him to help me. I couldn't understand why I was in a place of no peace, no joy, no help, no money, no mother, and no husband. That's when the Spirit of God began to minister to my broken spirit in the words of a song by Jennifer Holiday called "To Teach Me."

God was allowing me to go through the rough places so that He could teach me to depend on Him. I knew if my mom had still been alive, I would have moved back home to the security I felt when she was living. I would have moved back to Boston where I already had a support system in place that consisted of friends and family whom I would have depended on and put my trust in.

At home I wouldn't have to worry about anything, but because of where I was physically, mentally, and spiritually, I had no one to depend on and trust in but God! Through God's mercy, I learned forgiveness. Through God's grace, I learned faith. I am by no means saying that my mother died because God wanted to teach me to depend on and trust Him, but God took that horrible place I was in and turned it around and made it work for my good and His glory.

I can now see that God was with me all along. I remember there was a time in my life when all I would do was sit on my couch. Every evening after I put my children to bed, I would sit in the corner of my couch in the same place. I did that for so long I wore a groove in that spot on the couch. Then one night as I was sitting on the couch, I began to cry out to God again for help. I was actually questioning God. *Why do I have to be strong all the time? Why do I have to raise my children all alone?* I kept throwing out the questions, and it took a minute for me to realize that God had been answering my questions all along. The question and answer session went something like this:

Q. God, why do I have to do everything by myself?

A. Who am I?

Q. God I need someone in my life I can depend on!

A. Who am I?

Q. "When things go wrong in the house or with my car, who will help me?

A. Who am I?

Q. When the children get sick, who will help me care for them?

A. Who am I?"

Q. What about the bills, who will help me pay them?

A. Who am I?

Q. What about the times I get lonely or the times I need to talk to a friend?

A. Who am I?

Section 1: Faith Is a Journey

This went on until I realized that God was reassuring me (again) that I was not alone. Oh yes, He had me and everything that concerned me. Today my four children are all adults who are learning to put their trust in God, like I had to and still do. Today my questions have turned into statements: "Okay, God, you said to train my children up in the way they should go, and when they are older they won't depart from it." So no matter what my children do, I know they have the Word of God in them! God's Word says that no weapon formed against them or me shall prosper, so as I lay down at night, I trust God to keep me and my family safe. I now say, "All things work together for good to them that love God, to them who are the called according to his purpose" (Romans 8:28 KJV).

I remind myself that God hasn't given me a spirit of fear, but of love, power, and of a sound mind. I know that God has given me not only the power but the authority to cast out demons and trample over serpents. I believe that God is a not man that He should lie, and I believe that every promise, every word in the Bible is true. If I put my trust in Him, God will take care of me and never leave me. God says that He has a plan for my life: to prosper me and not to harm me.

I am learning to look in the mirror and smile at the image I see because I was fashioned in His image and I am the righteousness of God through Christ Jesus. God promised that the righteous would never beg for bread. God has taken my messed up situations and turned them around for my good. He has restored my joy and peace. There are still times when I feel perplexed, but I know I'm not forsaken. I believe and trust that God is the Great I Am, the Creator of all things. I don't have to worry about the enemy because he is under my feet. Even though I still go through rough places, I know I walk in victory, not just because I am blessed and highly favored but because the promises of God are yes and amen. Another thing that helps me is knowing that God knew me before I was formed in my mother's womb, so all I have to do is believe, receive, and walk this life out!

As we walk by faith, ponder these thoughts; Remember the promises and the Provider! In other words, consider the source and act accordingly. I am not afraid to approach my Father, whom I call Daddy, Friend, Comforter, Brother, Sister, Provider, Defender, Peace, Strength, Husband, Mother, and *Teacher*!

Section 1: Faith Is a Journey

Ariel Jones is an alumnus of Lipscomb University with a B.A. in Journalism and New Media. She enjoys the simple things in life: God, family, friends, a good book or comic book, singing, humor, poetry and other hobbies. She is a published poetess and is currently working on a book of poetry that will be published in the near future. Ariel is also an aspiring actress and has been involved in several church plays and had the opportunity to perform at TPAC (Tennessee Performing Arts Center). She wouldn't be able to do anything without a great support system at home which includes a mother, father, and a younger brother. Her father, who transitioned to be with the Lord, pushed Ariel to be her best self and desired for her to whole heartedly seek the Lord as one who searches for water in a dry place. It is Ariel's prayer to be in line with God's Word and to have a heart for His people.

A Simplistic Faith

Ariel Jones

I'm a church girl. I grew up in the church and have been preached to, and preached at, more times than I can count. I've been anointed over, prayed over, and declared over too. I've heard all the church sayings to keep believers uplifted and could probably write a book of church sayings and make some money! I even sing in the church choir,

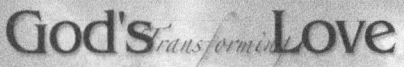

but none of that matters. During my Christian walk I am realizing my faith in God's word and personal relationship with God is most important.

The "church sayings" are alive in my life today, and sometimes gets me through a day when I think there is not a sign of hope left in my circumstances. It's those church sayings that help me smile through a test. I used to poke fun at them and repeat them like certain members of the church, but little did I know that I would be holding on to some of those same sayings years down the road.

I've always heard the saying, "Do you believe that with God nothing is impossible?" As a child and a new Christian, I would answer wholeheartedly, "Yes!" and receive a treat for answering so enthusiastically and correctly, of course. "Yes" was the right answer, but my yes, was not seasoned. I didn't really have the experience to back up the answer. As a new Christian, I didn't understand what that really meant until I went to college. That's when the question "Do you believe that with God nothing is impossible?" became real to me. It became as real as life itself.

Financially, college looked impossible. My parents and I didn't know where the money would be coming from because it just wasn't there. My grades were good, but not good enough to get a full ride to a local college, Lipscomb University. That's when I put my faith to work and called a meeting with God and shared my heart with Him. I told God that I didn't get accepted at Lipscomb University for nothing and that I believed that He would send the money to me and my family. I didn't know when or how the money would come, but I told Him that I knew He would make a way.

I had seen God work before in my family when my father was very ill. I was young then, but I knew somehow God would work it out. I really believed He would, and He did. Today my father is healed and serving the Lord. Just simply knowing that He could heal my father gave me hope. And guess what? God provided the financial resources for my college education. It used to surprise me when God blessed me, but not anymore. That's just the way He works! God has a track record I can easily trust. He is just great like that.

My last semester of college was the easiest and hardest semester at the same time. I was taking four classes that I loved in my major and minor, but then there was physics. The moment I found out that I had to take physics, I went into prayer mode. I just prayed I would pass. I didn't care if I passed one point higher than an F. That was my prayer the summer before my last semester. I made sure to do my part when the semester started. I built a relationship with the teacher, I took precise notes, and I studied continuously.

The first few exams I took I received Cs, which raised a shout on the inside of me. A couple of times I got cocky, and then I failed two tests, which caused sad days. I immediately repented and told God that I knew that I wasn't doing anything in this class using my own strength. The final exam approached, and I had to prepare His way. I had to graduate. *I had to*! I had come too far to let one class stop me from walking across that stage and receiving my diploma. I prayed and put it all in God's hands.

I was one of the last ones to leave the exam room, but I didn't care. I wanted to take my time to check and recheck my answers and possibly rework them. I didn't feel confident about the test, and I was at a loss for a moment. So what did I do? I treated myself to Starbucks, and I was still determined to trust in God till the end. He had promised me I would make it and I trusted Him.

A couple of days after the exam I tried to convince myself to skip out on what I thought was going to be a horror office visit with my professor. I found the nerve to approach my physics professor shortly after remembering a church saying, "God, will bring you through." I knocked and he answered. After exchanging pleasantries, I squeaked out my question and concern about my final grade. The professor showed me my test; it was a C! Not only did I pass the exam, but I passed the class, too, with a C! The first thing that popped out of my mouth was, "That's nothing but God" . . . another church saying.

I left my professor's office and went to the bathroom. I paced the floor and praised God. All I said the whole time was, "Glory to God!" over and over; it was one of those church sayings that actually became real to me. I called my mom who is a teacher, and she and the kids shouted in the classroom in excitement. I called Dad, and he shouted too. I couldn't call my brother Josh because he was at work, but I texted him the good news anyway. Then a song by Kevin Terry popped in my head. I found "Didn't I Tell You" on my iPod and played it a couple of times. I was that excited. It's a wonder that nobody came into the bathroom to see what I was doing. I know I was in there for a good hour. I've learned if you don't know how it's going to work out, you're in the right place for God to work! And God worked it for me! I know He'll do the same for you. Just as I had to trust God for my father's healing and my college finances, I am learning as I move into adulthood to trust God in every situation. I really do believe now nothing is impossible with God!

The question then becomes: How can I keep my faith strong? You are not me, and I am not you, but this may help sharpen your faith. Music is my life, so I listen to specific gospel songs in a playlist that literally preach to me when I may be in a troubling situation. Those songs uplift my spirit, and I remember how God's track record is above and beyond legit. I realize that if He did it before, He can do it again. He's able! Mighty God, You hold my world in Your hands!

Section 1: Faith Is a Journey

Regina Conley-Hockett is a native of Nashville, Tennessee. She is the wife of Charles Lee Hockett and has one son, Dejuan Eugene Conley. She is the daughter of the late Elder Fred Conley and Willodes Conley Thompson. Regina is well known in Nashville, Tennessee, for her testimony of forgiveness after the tragic death of her twelve-year-old daughter, Adriane Dickerson. Regina is also president and CEO of Victorious Mothers of Murder, a support group that was birthed after her daughter's death. Regina has been providing support groups, retreats, and one-on-one counseling to families throughout the Nashville area. Victorious Mothers of Murder has several mothers who have joined Regina in her effort to reach families nationwide.

The mission of Victorious Mothers of Murder is to counsel, encourage, and provide a support system to share how we can be overcomers and victorious when we go through the process of grief after a violent loss. Regina says, "Violence affects families and communities in a very tragic way." She believes if we start early with violence prevention services, families will not have to experience the emotional stress that violent behaviors puts on families and communities.

She is a member of Born Again Church Christian Outreach Ministries, where her pastors are Bishop Horace and Kiwanis Hockett.

God's Transforming Love

Just When I Thought This Chapter Was Closed

Regina Conley-Hockett

Nineteen years ago my life was turned upside down from the tragic loss of a gift from God that I fervently prayed for . . . a daughter. Adriane Nicole Dickerson was born May 10, 1983. The Lord allowed me to have her for 12 years (not long enough for me), but His ways and thoughts are not like ours. It was during the heartbreaking loss of the life of my baby girl, a living doll, when I learned how to hold on to my faith, as both my immediate and church family prayed, loved, and encouraged me through the transition. God's peace draped me like a security blanket that enabled me to stand in those times of depression and during the thoughts of suicide.

I long for my child's presence. But I learned that through this process, great suffering is an indication of the proof of one's unshakable trust in God. The foundation of my faith was being tested. My faith in God during the course of life was on a roller-coaster ride. Even so, it was maintained through times of trial as well as times of blessings. It is during times of adversity that the reflection of God shines brightest. This kind of faith reflects God's nature in us. No matter what we face in life, during those times we can trust that God is in control. We must rely on Him and on His goodness.

When I thought the chapter in my life dealing with my daughter's death was closed, I received an e-mail concerning her trial—a trial that lasted a little more than eight years. I was still healing through the grief of losing my daughter, who was murdered at the tender age of 12. When I received the message in November 2009, it seemed apparent that a discrepancy was discovered. I was requested to follow-up in the office the next day. Not knowing what to expect, I immediately started to pray, hoping something would be revealed through the Holy Spirit. (That's what I do when I need answers from my Daddy God). I don't know if I missed His response or if I had to wait until I arrived at the meeting to know the answer because I heard nothing from God.

After hearing the news that there was a glitch in one of the testimonies—yes, perjury—my emotions were all over the place, but I sensed the Spirit of Jesus' peace come over me. It was a transformation of love that manifested in calmness. I realized this issue was so much bigger than me. What did it mean? Were they going to release the trigger man? Would justice be rendered completely?

I have experienced God's love often when I come to a place where the situation is out of my hands. I call those times a God-size kind of job. I recognized this thing was not my battle. I had to activate my measure of faith. I had the faith to continue to walk in forgiveness as God molded more compassion in me.

To have faith means more than just to believe. (Hebrews 11:1 NKJV) defines faith as "the substance of things hoped for, the evidence of things not seen". When people believe that God will fulfill His promise, they are showing true faith, even when they don't now see evidence. Faith keeps you moving forward despite what you don't see or feel. It is trusting in the character of God, believing His promise, and knowing His rewards are sure.

When adversity knocks at your door—and it surely will—use God's formula: "Fill your minds with those things that are good and that deserve praise: things that are true, noble, right, pure, lovely, and honorable. Put into practice what you learned and received from me, both from my words and from my actions. And the God who gives us peace will be with you" (Philippians 4:8–9 GNT). In the midst of hardship and trials, God teaches us to see the situation from His perspective. He adjusts our thinking, our attitudes, and our goals. We are

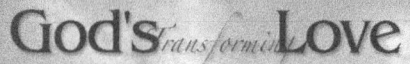

spiritually joined to Jesus, and we now have perpetual access to God's grace and to His unmerited favor. We have to turn to Him for forgiveness and help. Refuse to deny Him, refuse to quit, refuse to give in, and refuse to "curse God and die" (Job 2:9 GNT).

Know that the faith inside us is real and can't be shaken. Now I know why James says, "My brethren, count it all joy when ye fall into divers temptations; Knowing this, that the trying of your faith worketh patience. But let patience have her perfect work, that ye may be perfect and entire, wanting nothing" (James 1:2–4 KJV). Know that tribulation will come, but it won't win. The suffering won't destroy us; it can only strengthen us. This verse has become one of my many favorite Scripture verses. If you're needing a word of prayer, read this out loud:

> *Father, I come before You in the name of Jesus, and I choose life today! I will walk in faith and not in fear. Because the Lord is on my side, I will not fear what any man can do to me. Father, in the name of Jesus, I ask You to open my eyes to any hidden areas of fear in my life. Lord, Your Word says faith comes by hearing the Word of God, and I will build up my faith today by reading Your Word, speaking it, declaring it, and acting upon it. Thank You, Father, for the hedge of protection that You bring in response to my faith. Thank You that through the righteousness of Jesus, I can confidently trust in Your peace and safety for my life and home, knowing that Your angels are always on guard. I believe today! In Jesus' name, I pray. Amen.*

Section 1: Faith Is a Journey

Gwendolyn E. Google is a retired, exceptional education teacher of 30-plus years. She feels that teaching is her life-long calling and passion, as she has ministered to young people of all ages, at school through the Fellowship of Christian Athletes and at home during meals around the kitchen table. "Mama Google," as she is affectionately known, continues to enjoy these relationships that God has put together over the years. Gwen looks forward to spending special times with her four adult children: Brice, Raymond, Regina, and Reggie Jr., who have been a great encouragement and support of her writing. Being a grandmother is an exciting part of Gwen's life, and she enjoys times with her nine grandchildren who know her as G-Ma. Gwen also feels blessed to have her mother, Jean Mackey, enjoying this season of her life with her, having mother-daughter, talks, shopping, and bonding. Gwen plans to take some pleasurable trips to other countries beginning with the Holy Land. Gwen also plans to continue writing books to encourage and help families and to write children's literature books.

Until Death Do Us Part

Gwendolyn E. Mackey-Google

I know sharing my experience—the experience of losing a loved one, and, in my case, the loss of my husband—will help someone else. Writing about the subject of my husband's death has been extremely

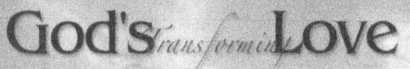

emotional. There were many times I had to stop and didn't want to start again. I reminded myself, *it's not about you, Gwen. It's about what God wants you to do!* Keeping this in mind aided in my comfort and strength to complete writing my story.

Standing next to my husband's hospital bed where he had been for a few weeks fighting liver disease, I started thinking about the vows we'd made: until death do us part. These vows stared me in the face. After 31 years of marriage and 36 years of a relationship, it could be over. *God I trust you with his life!* What can I do? I gave my husband permission to go. I told him we would be okay . . . but would we?

The nurse entered the room, saying something; it was a blur.

I asked, "What did you say?"

She said, "This is the end."

I thought, "*It can't be."* I felt like I was walking in a fog. Was this a dream or reality?

"He is gone," were the words from the nurse's mouth.

I felt such a peace and knew God was holding me in his arms. The doctors said, "He was a great man and it was a pleasure to know him." I only heard bits and pieces of conversations. It was difficult to digest. However, with the memories I shared with my husband, Reggie, and the relationship I had with the Lord both gave me hope that I would make it.

A day does not go by that I don't think of my beloved husband, Elder Reginald Google. Reggie and I met at his sister's house. She lived across the street from me. He was a freshman in college, and I was a senior in high school. It was Christmas-time, and we both were on school break. He asked his sister to call me over so he could meet me. I went over to the house, not knowing what she wanted.

When I arrived, his sister opened the door and said, "Someone wants to meet you." She introduced me to Reggie. We stood talking for a little while, and then he pointed out to me that we were standing under the mistletoe. I was a little reluctant to allow him to kiss me, but I finally did. I was expecting a small peck on the check. Instead, he gave me a full-fledged French kiss! *Wow!* I'd never been kissed like that before. He asked for my number, and the rest is history.

During our next visits, he told me how he and his brother-in-law talked about me and watched me as I walked home each day. Reggie had planned the entire encounter under the mistletoe. It worked. Like most couples, we had ups and downs in our relationship. Neither of us were committed Christians at the time, but we attended church together. There was a time when Reggie and I had broken up, but he continued to attend church. Although he wasn't as committed as some, Reggie had many powerful encounters with God. One of those encounters happened the day I accepted Jesus as my Lord and Savior. He told me later, when I went to the altar, the Lord told him that I was his wife. Reggie told God, "No!"

Five years later, Reggie committed his life to God and asked me to marry him. We prayed about everything that was related to our wedding, and I do mean *everything*. God gave us the date, place, and time. We were married June 26, 1976. The ceremony was heaven sent. The song before the ceremony was "Thank You Lord" by Walter Hawkins. The recessional song was "To God Be the Glory" by Andraé Crouch.

During Reggie's funeral, my brother shared words of comfort about our wedding. My brother remembered the big smile on Reggie's face as he walked me down the aisle to give me away. He said a feeling of uncertainty crossed his mind . . . what was behind the smile as he was about to give me to be wed.

The most memorable moment that I cherished during the wedding was the commitment we made to each other: until death do us part. As we left the church and stepped outside the door, the photographer requested us to kiss one more time. Reggie kissed me the same way he did under the mistletoe five years before, when it all began.

In penning this work, I reminisced many events of our lives: graduations, the wedding of our oldest son, birth of grandchildren, death of loves ones, and family reunions. However, losing Reggie has taught me to trust God's sovereignty the most. Reggie, the love of my life, passed October 24, 2007, three days after his birthday. His service was November 2 on my brother's birthday—the same brother who gave me away 31 years prior.

It was after the burial when snippets of reality came. Reggie was never returning home. How would I face this separation? It was the final parting of our physical bodies, but not our hearts. In those moments, I thought, *"How can I survive this separation?"* Unlike like a divorce when you can see each other occasionally, this separation on earth was final. It's so hard. The feelings of hurt, insecurity, abandonment, loneliness, and even anger flooded my entire being. Questions flooded my mind: Why did God allow him to leave? He could have said, no. Why weren't our prayers answered for healing? How can love hurt so bad?

During this transition of life, others helped me experience God's transforming love. For example, my godfather had just lost his wife a month before Reggie's death. He called me during a tumultuous period of grieving and told me if I accepted Reggie's death, it would be easier, and if I didn't, it would be harder! I appreciated his wisdom and tried to accept Reggie's death, one day at a time. That's all I could deal with. He was right; it made it a little easier. Although I faced difficulty during the next few months to a year grieving, I began to see the manifestation of God's love as I intentionally watched the hand of God in my life and our four children and their families. It was visible; my children began to transform into their purpose and destiny as Reggie had spoken into their lives.

Immediately after the funeral, my children and I received love and support from everywhere. Reggie was well loved by people near and far. Soon the people were gone, and I felt abandoned. I didn't understand why everyone was leaving me. I was forced into daily living as usual. I later learned during a counseling session that people were going back to their normal lives. This didn't feel normal to me, but I eventually understood.

My mother stayed with us for a few more weeks after Reggie's service, so I had someone with whom to talk. My dad died when I was five years old, and my mother raised four children with God's help, along with a loving and caring family, so I was sure she knew what I was going through. Dad was killed in a car accident not far from our home. My mother was young and pregnant with my baby sister. I asked my mother how she dealt with my father's death. Mom told me she was able to survive, even without remarrying, because she choose to place priority on raising her children, which motivated her to continue with life.

My children and I were there for each other for some time, but now they are grown, either in college or gone to live their own lives. Many times I was left alone to deal with this state of separation, with the new responsibilities—those Reggie handled. I was also left with a sense of marriage without the other person. I often found myself waiting for his return to assist with those household husband duties, and then I would realize he was not coming home.

I had never been in that state of mind before. I talked to God and to myself all the time. I also played praise and worship music to help the atmosphere in my home to stay peaceful. I found I needed adult interaction, but most of my friends were married, divorced, or single, as a widow I didn't know how to relate in those settings. In learning to hear God in reshaping my life, a few members of my church suggested grief share counseling. The recommendation was welcomed at that time in my life. I was willing to try if it would help me through this process. Grief share was very beneficial for me, as well as for my children. I learned that grief is a process. Secondly, I didn't have to be afraid, and lastly I was not alone. The Scripture verse that has been my mantra comes from Hebrews 13:5b–6: (NKJV), For He Himself has said, "I will never leave you nor forsake you." So we may boldly say: "The LORD *is* my helper; I will not fear. What can man do to me?"

The time came for me to return to work. I wasn't sure I was ready to deal with this situation. Being at home was a safe place. I didn't have to talk about Reggie's passing unless I desired to. I knew my students would have questions and want to discuss what happened. "In all your ways acknowledge Him, and He shall direct your paths" was the Scripture verse that came to my mind, helping me to remember to trust in God and not my feelings (Proverbs 3:6, NKJV). I also began another level of self-care by returning to a local gym to work out and joined a prayer group that brought balance back to my life. I still had moments of uncertainty but learned to seek out fun and to enjoy life. The cornerstone for me was to acknowledge God first in everything for direction. It was as if God became my husband to help with decision making as in Isaiah 54 (KJV).

One of the most difficult times for me was returning home after work, especially on Fridays. Dealing with the weekends and being home alone most of the time became a great challenge. I remember one evening I walked into our bedroom and felt very uncomfortable. I recognized the spirit of fear was trying to come upon me. I recognized this fear and decided to resist it and declared the Scripture. The power of God came over me, and I told that spirit it had to leave in the name of Jesus. I pleaded the blood of Jesus over my house and told the spirit of fear to leave and never return. A peace came into the room, and my house has since been peaceful every day.

There is no question that I have experienced the powerful prayer of the saints sustaining me. It was the same power that kept me from the time of Reggie's transition until now! Agreement in prayer is truly the greatest force on earth that works every time. Having a personal relationship with God and a prayer life was a significant component in helping me go through this season of life. I have prayed many prayers, crying out to God, listening to what He says and obeying Him. It wasn't easy, but I learned to make time to commune with my Father God daily, which was and is a great necessity.

My next challenge would be getting through the holiday seasons. Since my children and close family members lived in different cities and states, we normally spent Thanksgiving in our individual homes and came together for Christmas. The first holiday, one month after Reggie's death, was Thanksgiving and then Christmas was upon us. I am thankful we all were able to spend both holidays together, which was truly a blessing, providing support and also keeping the tradition and enjoying the memories as one.

If there are any regrets I have it is that Reggie and I didn't talk more and how I wish we had laughed more during his illness. We needed to discuss the future. I needed to know what his desires were about living and dying. We did manage to have a will in place before the chaos of illness. Having things in order can be a great weight lifted off of you during the care-taking of a spouse.

Culturally, we learned not to talk about what to do if one is possibly dying; going home to be with the Lord; because it might seem as though one is in doubt and lacking faith. It is important that we understand that during moments of terminal illness that permission for freedom to talk is viewed as God-ordained time of preparation, not doubt. It affords both individuals opportunity to share their wishes far after they have transitioned.

Reggie and I talked about healing and deliverance and not about what to do if he went home to be with the Lord. We didn't talk about his desires or feelings in terms of being tired or perhaps being ready to go with the Lord. We both kept proclaiming the faith of healing. I did, the kids did, but somewhere along the way Reggie made his choice, unknown to us, to be with his Lord and Savior. During life transitions, such as terminal illnesses, it is important to remember God has the ultimate decision. So talk and give space to hear the hearts of your loved ones. It is not an act of faithlessness.

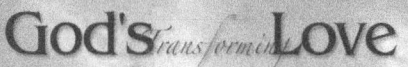

I would like to share my last words to my husband with you:

Dear Reginald,

Today as I reflect on our marriage vows—for better or worse, in sickness and health, till death do us part—who knew we would fulfill them too soon. I'm happy we made the most of the times that we had—all the family trips, reunions, the blessings of four beautiful children and four grandchildren, who have been the joy of our lives. I can only smile as I'm sure you are smiling. I'm a little sad now, but having the assurance that I will see you again strengthens me day by day. Our family Scripture verse from Matthew 6:33 (NKJV)—"But seek first the kingdom of God and His righteousness, and all these things shall be added to you"—has, and will take me and the family through this time. Your leadership as a godly husband, father, elder, and prophet will always be treasured and remembered.

Your transition was glorious and peaceful; we couldn't ask for more, but for you to return. When I called you back, you chose to stay with the Lord. I accepted your choice because I believe it is God's way. I love you more than you'll ever know. Oh, yes, I did tell you so. So rest from your labor and enjoy your new life. I'll see you in the future.

Lovingly,

Gwennie Pooh, Your wife

Presently, I have been propelled into a new season in my life. Retirement! I am excited about what God has for me in my new season. Finally, I want to recommend for you prayer, grief share groups, and, if necessary, professional counseling to obtain balance in your new life. For those who are in a marriage covenant, "never put off till tomorrow what you can do today". May you have faith and trust in God for

Section 1: Faith Is a Journey

the journey. It's important to enjoy your spouse every day, hour, and minute of your life. Learn to agree to disagree! Always be ready to say I'm sorry, and enjoy making up! Remember you are making memories daily, and try to limit regrets. Make happy memories!

I can truly sing the song with joy played prior to our wedding ceremony and during the funeral recession: Thank you, Lord, for all You have done for me!

"Grief never ends, but it changes.

It is only a passage, not a place to stay.

Grief is not a sign of weakness nor a lack of faith.

It is the sign of love."

Author Unknown

Rev. Lalita R. Smith, is a prophetic journalist, songwriter, poet, author, editor, minister, and Christian publishing consultant, who has been writing by inspiration for more than 35 years. She has dedicated the past three decades to offering assistance to various Christian writers who have been seeking guidance, leadership, and editorial assistance. She assists in bringing their God-inspired works to the marketplace. After relocating to Nashville from Southern California, she became a member of the Spirit Lead Writers Network while a member of Born Again Church.

She is an active member at Gateway Church in Southlake, Texas, under the leadership of Pastors Robert and Debbie Morris and is a regular participant at Glory of Zion with Dr. Chuck Pierce, in Corinth, Texas. For more information and to purchase her available products please visit: http://www.havilahhouse.weebly.com and http://www.patreon.com/Lalita

Transformation by Multiple Transitions

Lalita R. Smith

Transitions occur in everyone's life. They are a natural part of living, growing, changing, and dying. We transition from childhood into

Section 1: Faith Is a Journey

teenagers, into adults and then into the elderly. We move usually as children at least one or two times, forcing changes in friends, neighborhoods, churches, teachers, and schools.

However, in my life, I've experienced an unusually high number of transitions, approximately 45-50, and that is 45-50 more than I ever wanted or expected. My personal transitions have occurred far more times than what happens on average. Through so many transitions, from city to city, from the East to the West Coast and back again, I have experienced many things that have helped to shape me into the woman that I am today.

I want to share with you briefly the building of my faith, courage, and trust in God, which was the result of my personal spiritual journey and multiple life transitions. In hind's sight, I want to give you some wisdom. I want to impart some consolations as well, and I promise to be open and honest in sharing how I contributed to this kind of lifestyle.

Let me start by asking this question. Are all transitions God-ordained? Are some moves the result of our own rebellion, stubbornness, wrong speech, and willful choices? I believe the answer is a combination of all of these. There are times in our lives when we are directed by the Lord to make a move as a means to advance the kingdom of God on earth. Our spouses' job or our own may require one and those are certainly to be embraced.

Look at the children of Israel, for example, who were told to move with the cloud of God's glory repeatedly. As a result, they had to break camp continuously during their 40 years of sojourning in the wilderness, even after being miraculously delivered out of the land of Egypt.

What is God's greater purpose in it all? I believe the answer to this question is to build faith, give hope, and test our trust in Him. How many of you too have said, "Thy kingdom come, thy will be done in my life?" Did you mean it sincerely? If so, then we all have to resolve to obey Him, no matter what He may require of us. When we do, our experiences then become the testimonials of hope that will reach others who

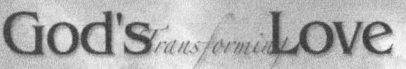

are undergoing major transitions in life but may be becoming weary.

I can't tell you how many times I became weary in my journey. "Oh, no, not again Lord," I would retort every time I heard Him say, "Pack, it's time to move." I knew it meant within a short amount of time, generally six months to a year on average, that I would have to pack up all my belongings and move forward again.

Emotionally, it was challenging. Physically, it was exhausting, but once I yielded my will, to the will of the Lord, I would immediately pray and ask my angels to direct me to free boxes. To exhibit my faith in the Lord's plan for me, especially when He did not tell me where I was going next, I immediately packed my first box of books or valuables, that I knew I would not need again until much later. That one act of faith began to set blessings in motion in the spirit realm. It gave the Lord tangible proof of my faith, submission and trust in Him.

Next, I put my operation for success plan into motion. I want to share that with you right now. It has been used repeatedly and has helped me to literally eliminate the overwhelming sense of stress that envelopes moving.

Formula for Moving Forward Successfully:

If you have found yourself in a place of transition and can't seem to move forward as successfully as you might wish to, take a look at these points and be sure you have set things in divine order. As you take these steps, you will find it easier and more pleasant to handle life's transitions.

Step #1: Yield your will to the will of the Lord. "If ye be willing and obedient, ye shall eat the good and the fat of the land." (Isaiah 1:19 KJV). In order to move forward, you must first allow God to be GOD in your heart.

Step #2: Unload Unnecessary Baggage: "Forgive us our debts as we forgive those who trespass against us." (Matthew 6:12 KJV) As you sort, pack and discard old things, do the same emotionally, and financially, where possible. Release all former debts and debtors from your past. Peacefully sever all ties from the experiences you had in this place, and leave clean, healthy cuts in associations on every level where possible. This keeps all channels of divine supply open and flowing into your life.

Step #3: Embrace Your New Location: Research your new destination, city, country, church, school, etc. and begin making a new roadmap of things you will do. Compile a list of the places you will visit. Get excited about this new leg of your spiritual journey. Set some personal goals and make some exciting plans.

Step #4: **Make New Connections:** Reach out to new people everywhere, the grocery store, the dry cleaners, the bank, etc. You will be amazed at the number of quality people the Lord will put in your pathway and begin to connect you to. Join a Meet Up group, a hobby group, a writer's group, even before you arrive and begin making some new friends. Remember, he who would have friends must first show himself friendly.

Never forget that your destiny is always before you, ahead of you. Surprisingly, we never know who the next key connector will be. But God does know, and He orders the footsteps of the righteous so that His plans, will, and purposes come forth.

Transitions Facilitate Growth

Why did the Lord need me to move so many times? I believe many of my moves involved Him using me to go into other people's homes, as a prophet, servant, witness, helper, comforter, and friend. There were many people I went to *serve*, whom I helped to organize their lives in the natural and to help them spiritually also.

There were live-in situation's that allowed me to be the answer to a saint's prayers like: "Lord, if you bless me with a big house, I promise I will be a blessing to Your people." So, the Lord decided to try their hearts and their words. In many of my instances, the people who had spoken those words were not aware that they were being tested, but I was because the Lord would let me know. Some passed, and some failed!

I believe some transitions were to help me build a strong, viable kingdom network of friends and ministry supports and give me a future audience for my writings. I am still so blessed by the number of people who will send me a note, thanking me for how the Lord may have used me when our paths crossed. These notes, cards, and e-mails are priceless mementos of my struggles, faith, and obedience during some very difficult and painful experiences.

Trust me when I tell you this: not any one of my transitions was easy, especially not right after my divorce when my son, Nicholas, had to spend six months on a friend's couch or living room floor. At another time, he spent nine months in his sleeping bag at the foot of my bed in a friend's house in Los Angeles. But all those times allowed us to bond together as mother and son. It enabled us to become friends and prayer partners who learned how to enter into agreement with heaven to see our needs met on earth. They were precious times that I will always treasure.

We both learned how to *serve* the families we lived with. God taught us to humbly care for others even during our most difficult and unpleasant circumstances. It built compassion and mercy in us as well as gratefulness and trust in the Lord. We grew in compassion for God's people as well.

Often I had to wait for money, transportation, and the next "open door" in our living situation. For example, while still in southern California after our mobile home went into foreclosure, (well. that's part of another testimony). Nick and I spent the night in our van in the streets of Malibu. Yet God in His faithfulness, eventually opened up a door of employment for me in the heart of Malibu. It was sooooooooo beautiful there!

We soon moved into a home that was fifteen miles up a hill in Malibu Canyon. Why did the Lord take us to such a remote location? He had a need and an assignment for my son. He needed Nick to share the Gospel message of salvation with a young man. The owner of the house we rented rooms from had a son who had moved from New York about a month after we moved in. He and Nick became friends quickly. Nick invited him to our church, and then walked him through the plan and prayer of salvation. He received the Lord and very quickly thereafter, we moved forward to an apartment in Van Nuys. Why was it time to move? We had accomplished the Lord's assignment for my son.

In that apartment, we had a number of prayer meetings and were hosts to a homeless family of five who had moved from New York to California. We took in a homeless artist named Cindy, with her cat, who later became my art mentor. During this same time period, we hosted another homeless woman named Rebeca, who was a budding fashion designer.

We learned the importance of demonstrating the gift of hospitality as Believers and not just being the recipients of the hospitality of others. We were more sensitive to the needs of other people who came to live with us. We saw that we were not the only ones who had to endure a season of struggle in life. We learned not to be too demanding or pushy about how much time was required for them to become strong enough to move forward. This is so critical to understand. Why? Because humanly speaking, we have our individual timetable and expectation of people in circumstances like this. However, the Lord has a timetable that is right, and it oftentimes does not line up with ours, as His requires a longer recovery period. It takes great grace to allow our heavenly Father's timetable to rule over our own.

Overcoming the Fear of the Unknown

What was the biggest challenge or obstacle I had to overcome with every transition? The number one issue for me was the fear of the unknown. Not knowing where I was headed next, when my actual release would come, or how I would get there financially created a lot of stress. Over time, however, I learned to look those fears in the face and say, "My *God* is faithful. God has always come through for me! I filled the atmosphere with this scriptural confession: "I will trust in the Lord with my whole heart. I will not lean to my own understanding. In all my ways, I will acknowledge Him knowing that He will direct my path. I will trust in the Lord and not be afraid!" (Adapted from Proverbs 3:4-5 NKJV) That confession got me through those attacks of fear and doubt!

Handling What Other's Think

The number two lesson was learning how to handle other people's issues, challenges, and perspectives regarding my "homelessness." It is not easy for other believers to accept the place God has His servants and children in at times. They oftentimes expect you to just get up and make things happen for yourself, like they may be able to do. Yet, in my case, there have been times when I could not "make things happen." I had to wait upon and for the Lord.

When the owner said it was time to go, that became really challenging, especially when the Lord had not yet said the same thing to me. There were several times when I had nowhere to go and no money with which to make something happen. I had to ride out the time amid hostile emotional confrontations. I learned to be loving to my host in spite of their frustrations about my still being there, and took whatever steps I could to facilitate change. Eventually, as He does, the Lord worked all things together to the good of all concerned.

Enduring Personal Losses

The third greatest challenge was enduring the loss of my personal belongings and things I had collected over the years. What was most damaging and difficult to bear was the most recent loss of more than thirty years' worth of my inspirational writings when I did not have the money to pay for a storage unit. I had to leave them behind in Nashville after being told by the Lord to trust Him with a move to Dallas in 2013.

I trusted Him, moved in with my daughter, Angie, and two grandsons, Nathan and Joey, in Dallas, only to be abandoned by her within less than thirty days. Although, short it was great to spend time nurturing, preparing meals and serving my grandchildren . . . it was a tremendous blessing to my heart.

After their departure, it was a struggle for me to survive that first year in Texas because I had difficulty getting work, but with God's help and the support of many dedicated ministry donors—and an amazing new family of believers at Gateway Church (Southlake Campus)—I survived that transition. I am most grateful to be a Texan now.

What were my Mistakes?

I have to admit that I made some mistakes that cost me losses and forced transitions. The examples I am sharing are not a chronological account of my life. The biggest thing that got me into trouble was my mouth, my negative confession, even during times when I thought I was speaking faith. When you have a prophetic mouth, you have to train yourself to "watch what you say." Why? Because this world is governed by the spoken word. What you and I say really does have the power to change our circumstances, and sometimes, more rapidly than we can imagine.

For example, when I lived in the Piccadilly Apartment complex off Windsor Green in Goodlettsville, TN (several years prior to my move to Texas) I made the mistake of confessing to people who lived there *but were moving out* that I would be right behind them. Now, that was a **huge** mistake!

On the surface those words seemed innocent, but soon afterwards, my finances came under attack. I was no longer producing the income needed to maintain my stay there. Sure enough, I got the command from the Lord to pack but had no idea that I would find myself in a Tennessee courtroom undergoing an eviction proceeding, but I was.

Sometime later, after seeking the Lord about those unfortunate circumstances, He revealed to me a two-fold set up. My negative confession was one critical factor. The other was surprising. The Lord revealed to me that because of a future assignment in my life, He wanted me to know firsthand what many of His people went through

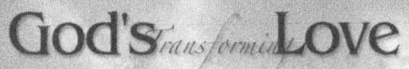

when lack of money, health issues, and loss or joblessness forced them to become evicted and homeless. My heart really did hurt that day in the courtroom—not so much for myself, but for so many others who had no hope in Jesus, no mercy or compassion from either their landlords or the US court system. Jesus, have mercy!

Greatest Lessons: Trust in God and Forgiveness

Adaptability to rules and lifestyle differences when you are in another person's space is another great lesson you undergo. We all grew up with different cultural beliefs, and the way we do things is sometimes the way we force others to become when they are in our space. Not allowing offenses to occur over minor differences of taste, style, and preference is another thing I learned during many transitions in living. I've learned that I must not take everything personally but be quick to forgive others who may offend me.

In closing, I just want to say this. Transitions enables growth in us on so many levels. Our appreciation for little things becomes heightened. A clearer understanding of who we are, and who others see us as, is gained. I realize now that I am a prophetic, "forerunner" – one whom the Lord sends ahead of others to learn -- so that the knowledge and information they share helps many others. I pray this testimony has blessed you.

So I urge you to learn to joyfully embrace each time of transition in your life. Hopefully, you will find that the Lord may just be giving you the opportunity to have your life filled with many wonderful experiences, lessons, blessings, and surprises.

Section 1: Faith Is a Journey

Wanda Hodge lives in Nashville Tennessee. Wanda lives and breathes to testify of God's grace and mercy toward her. Recently retired, she loves grand mothering her two grandchildren, singing in the choir, studying the word, cooking and extending a helping hand to those in need. From statistic to significance is the story of Wanda's life. She now uses her faith and life experience to encourage, inspire and to bring healing to others. Wanda is a woman of all seasons, in which she discovered to be Seasons of God and His Transforming love.

A Blessed Journey

Wanda Hodge

My name is Wanda Hodge, and I am an overcomer. I am a seasoned woman who has learned the true meaning of love and forgiveness. Recently retired, I enjoy loving and teaching my four grandchildren, singing in my church choir, reading, encouraging women not to give up, and ever learning new things. I am a woman who has been transformed through God's love for me when I couldn't love myself. I am healed, and my whole spirit, soul, and body are a channel for God's blessing.

Most eight-year-old little girls love surprises, adventure, and fun. Their innocence leads them to live in anticipation of becoming twelve,

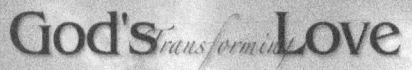

then fourteen, the long awaited sweet sixteen, and so on. However, this eight-year-old dreaded each new day she awoke alone, afraid, and ashamed. My stepfather had robbed my innocence at that age, and the abuse continued until I was nineteen. I always felt alone and looked for something, a clue that I could compare with what was happening to me. I desperately wanted to talk to someone, but who? How? When? What would I say? I finally resigned myself to the thought and lie that this happened to all girls my age and kept my secret to myself.

I had accepted Christ in my heart at the age of eleven. Easter was always special to me. The Easter of my twelfth birthday I decided it was time to tell my mother what was happening. I did not know what to expect. She listened and showed no emotion. By this time my mother had given birth to three other children. When my mother confronted my stepdad about the sexual abuse, he became furious and vehemently denied my accusations. After the conversation, he took my mother and three siblings away in the car. I was left alone. I cried until I could cry no more. The conversation never came up again, however, my stepdad continued the sexual abuse for seven more years. At the age of fifteen, I started working. Between working after school and being a latchkey kid, I felt a little independence, and it was a good feeling until I had to return to the prison of abuse.

At the age of eighteen, I became pregnant by a young man who was not my stepfather. I was working but still in high school. My mom kept my baby girl. I stayed away from home as much as I could until my stepdad ordered me to come to the club he operated when I got off work at night. When I turned twenty, I moved in with a girlfriend who had an apartment. My mother refused to let me take my baby with me. I spent the next five years working and looking forward to the day when I would be able to take care of my baby. That finally happened when she was five years old. I took my child when my mother was not home. I worked hard and enrolled in training classes to better myself and situation.

Section 1: Faith Is a Journey

I became pregnant again and gave birth to my son. I loved my children and was determined to make a home for them. No sacrifice was too great. During this time, I became a licensed cosmetologist. I also completed training to be a forklift operator. I worked with children and seniors, and later became a massage therapist. Most of the time I maintained two jobs. Life for me was a struggle that consistently built my character. As time moved on, my children became teenagers and finally adults. Both are purpose focused, and I am truly proud of them.

Just when I thought I could work, begin to save, and pursue other interests, my health became a challenge—so much so that it cost me my employment. I found myself again alone, afraid, and ashamed. It was not long before I was homeless and became a resident at the women's mission. I knew in my mind and heart that God had not left me. The mission was my blessing. It was through their clinic that the journey of my diagnosis with breast cancer began. I lived at the mission for the next six months. When I left, I went to one of my Christian sister's home, where I was welcomed and loved unconditionally. While, I continued a barrage of tests and referral appointments to determine what the lump was in my right breast.

Faced with a lump in my right breast, another possible health issue and no medical insurance, I knew without a shadow of doubt that God was with me. It was confirmed by mammogram and biopsy that it was breast cancer on February 14, 2013. What a bitter sweet gift. There I was, single and about to be one breast less. Tina Turner sung the song, "What's Love Got to Do with It?" For a moment, I thought the same thing. God, where are you . . . where is the love? I remember the blank feeling I had. Then I thought about crying, but asked myself what would I be crying about? I didn't have an answer.

Almost immediately, I remembered God's promise and His Word. He created me and He is my Healer. A peace engulfed me that I had long forgotten amidst all my other trials of life. Now, you may be thinking, *What a Valentine's gift to receive*. But my friend, that's exactly what it was. God transformed my thoughts and revealed His hand of provision during my treatment. It was a miracle of love just for me; everything I needed was granted by His grace. Each phase of the process of my healing demonstrated is divine grace and love. The medical team, my supportive family and friends, and even people I didn't know prayed and walked with me throughout the journey of my diagnosis, consultation, surgery, treatment and follow-ups.

After many consultations with doctors and through prayer, I chose the option of mastectomy. From that moment on, I considered myself a healed survivor in Jesus' name. I had already formed my conclusion: Breast Cancer is not my death sentence! I was ready for the journey.

My surgery was quick—approximately seven days after the diagnosis. It was on February 21, 2013. Family and friends were there, praying with me before surgery. In spite of circumstances, we were a loud and fun group. Nineteen lymph nodes were removed and four were found to be cancerous. The surgery was a success.

The healing process had begun. By then, I was so thankful. I found no reason to be sad about anything. For the first time in a long time, I felt my future was hopeful, even though I experienced a few complications as a result of diabetes, which prolonged the incisional healing. Nevertheless, in my heart I knew that God would not put more on me than I could bear. For example, a machine to aid in healing called a wound Vac was gifted to me from the clinic on my birthday. This machine assisted in the closure of my incision. The wound Vac ensured an environment to promote further healing, preventing another surgical procedure to close the area of surgical mastectomy and reconstruction. (A great gift, huh?)

Reflecting back on my journey, I have truly experienced the Giver of gifts, who keeps on giving. The great gift of love is evident in my life being transformed when I believed and accepted God's only Son. "For God so loved the world that He gave His only begotten Son, that whoever believes in Him should not perish but have everlasting life"

(John 3:16, NKJV).

I have experienced so many answered prayers during my time of doctor's visits, chemotherapy, and radiation. Please do not get me wrong; it was a rocky, stormy, and sometimes cold journey, but it was knowing that the presence of God's love and grace were with me through it all that I was able to see the sun shining brightly, guiding me through His Son.

In fact, the result of this journey has birthed new life in me. A new beginning. I have applied the following recipe to my daily spiritual journey. It is a poem titled "Spiritual Lemonade."

Spiritual Lemonade

Lemons: Take negative reports and trials of life, although sour

Sugars: Add God's Word to the situation; liven it up because life needs sweeteners

Water: Work in your faith, stirring vigorously with fervent prayer

Recommended Usage: Drink daily, or as often as needed.

My friends, if you're wondering when things will turn green again, just remember spring always comes after winter.

I believe that my positive attitude and trust in God unlocked the door to my answers to so many prayers. If I were given this journey again, I would welcome it with great joy just as before. "You are of God, little children, and have overcome them, because He who is in you is greater than he who is in the world." (1 John 4:4, NKJV)

Moment of Reflection

Lilly Lester

What is my description of faith?

Why is it difficult to exercise faith continuously?

How might my life be different if I walked by faith, and not by sight?

How do I respond when my faith is on trial?

How do I feed my faith and starve my doubts?

Section II

Restoration

Restoration

Lilly Lester

How many times has Satan tried to traumatize us through attacks of sickness, finances, family, relationships, doubt, fear, curses, etc.? These over used tactics are to steal our self-worth and trick us into a victim mentality. They cause us to take our eyes off the Greater One and gravitate toward the lesser, temporal things. We then find ourselves in need of restoration and healing.

Regardless of how unique our circumstances appears to be; Hebrews 13: 5-6 (NKJV) tells us "For He Himself has said "I will never leave nor forsake you". He loves us unconditionally. Because we are made in His image, we are valuable to Him. So much so, He took our infirmities and bore our sickness by suffering and dying for our sins on the cross. He lovingly waits for us to intentionally make a choice to trust Him to revive, reestablish, renew, heal and restore the broken, damaged, fragmented, barren pieces of our lives into one of His beautiful masterpieces. He still restores, heals, and transforms today.

In this section there are six stories that tell of miraculous healing and supernatural restorations. Each story paints a picture of total surrender to God's will, and a renewal of the mind.

He restores my soul; and leads me in the path of righteousness for his namesake. Psalms 23:3 (NKJV)

Section II: Healing and Restoration

Elder Karynthia A.G. Phillips is an author and ordained minister of the Gospel. Karynthia is bi-vocational as a minister and family practitioner. She is the Founder of Trinity Wholeness Ministries and works as a writers' coach for Spirit Lead Writers Network, which is based in Nashville, Tennessee. She is a freelance writer and speaker with three books to her credit. She has a passion for discipling others into spiritual maturity by the application of quiet time. It is her hope that her works will enlighten and clarify the position of authority and power available to Christians, as God's principles in Scripture are implemented each day.

Her desire is to see Christians pursue a life of wholeness through understanding the fullness of the gift of salvation. Her mantra: The unity of body, spirit, and soul are essential to fulfill the purpose of God for your life. She believes that balance via self-care is obtained as one develops a personal relationship with God through private worship, during quiet time and practicing a healthy lifestyle. She is a wife of 33 years, the mother of 3 adult children, and a grandmother to 2 granddaughters.

Crossroads to Personal Wholeness

By Karynthia Glasper-Phillips

This is what the LORD says: "Stand at the crossroads and look; ask for the ancient paths, ask where the good way is, and walk in it, and you will find rest for your souls."

(Jeremiah 6:16 NIV)

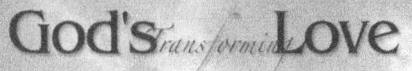

Crossroads to wholeness, my journey of learning self-care encompasses several years. At this juncture of life, I have found keys to achieving personal wholeness. Sure, I could talk about my hurts, illnesses, and many disappointments, but I want to take you down a different path to my restoration. Many of us have self-inflicted wounds, that are bleeding, and draining life out of us. We might not always be aware that this is happening internally, but the evidence is that there is very little joy, love, peace, or contentment manifesting in us. I believe the solution is to create a balanced life through self-care.

Jesus said the second greatest commandment after loving God with all your heart, soul, and mind is to, "Love your neighbor as yourself" (Matt. 22:39 NIV). The questions are: Do we love ourselves like we love our neighbors? Who are our neighbors? They are the people living next door, as well as people in our family, church, place of employment, and civic organizations. Stop for a moment. Answer a few reflective questions: "Are you honestly attending to your needs as you do for the needs of others?" What are some examples of your practices of self-care?

Although I don't know you, I suspect that you are giving a great deal of care and sacrificial love to your neighbors. I used to think doing things for myself was selfish, so I continually put others before my needs and wants. I thought, "After I finish this project I will get to me tomorrow." The problem was that other people's needs never stopped, so I never had time to get to me. The lesson I want you to learn from me is that you don't have to remain stuck in the mud of life. Jesus has more for us than joyless sacrificial living.

Women in America tend to have an unhealthy habit of self-denial, a form of neglect that leads to poor self-care and discontentment in every aspect of life. How can we serve, lead, or care for others if we neglect ourselves? Self-care is not selfishness. Self-care is learning to love yourself as you love your neighbors. Another way to say Matthew 22:39 is, *"Love yourself as your neighbor."* Acknowledging that

Section II: Healing and Restoration

we need and deserve more personal care is the beginning of personal wholeness.

I gave my life to Jesus in the eighth grade. Reading my Bible, fasting, and praying became all that I did because I wanted to attain spiritual maturity, Christlikeness, and intimacy with the Father God. I stopped hanging out with my girlfriends and enjoying life experiences like most young women my age. Some years after my spiritual transformation, I came to the crossroads and realized there was more to living a Christian life.

I sought answers for two questions: First, how can we thrive and enjoy life on earth if all we focus on is prayer, fasting, and reading scriptures? I was very glad to have my sins forgiven and enjoyed fellowship with God. But I found, that salvation offers wholeness in all aspects of our lives. There is more than forgiveness of sin. Self-care helps one to identify the fullness of the gifts God has provided. I discovered that although we are spiritual beings, we are also physical beings and God has created earthly as well as spiritual things for our enjoyment.

Second, amidst all the praying, fasting, and reading of scriptures, where was the sense of true sisterhood and unity among women in the church? I noticed there seemed to be a festering sore among the women in the choir, usher board, kitchen, and Sunday school. They just didn't seem to like each other. Regardless of the contention between the women, they always came together in a crunch to organize and successfully complete major tasks. I often wondered, and still do, what would happen if women laid aside their differences and pooled their gifts, talents, and resources? I believe there would be a huge shift globally impacting all facets of society.

Most of the Christian women I observed in church settings had similar characteristics: 1) They were tolerating one another instead of genuinely loving each other. 2) They criticized rather than celebrated one another's differences and God-given gifts and talents. 3) They were tired all the time, always had deadlines, and were curt. 4) They didn't take time to enjoy life.

There were a few women I observed who exemplified balanced lifestyles. They took care of themselves, accepted others as they were, served together, and mediated between women who disagreed. The balanced women in most cases appeared to be healthy spiritually, emotionally, and physically.

As I grew older, I observed that some women become neglectful of themselves for many reasons. For example, low self-esteem, gnawing wounds of the past, shame, unidentified talents, serving in the wrong capacity at church and work, minimal personal time, and lack of physical and mental exercise. When women are beyond overwhelmed with life's demands they do not adequately care for themselves, which inevitably immobilizes them at the crossroads of life.

I know all about this because I used to live that way. Yes I did. It wasn't until my "sister friend" had a conversation with me about my edginess and shortness that I realized how unhealthily out of balance my life was. She knew my heart to empower and love women, so she approached me in humility to get to the root of my behavior and empowered me to choose a better path.

Along my journey God has used young and seasoned women to help me wiggle out of my cocoon and transform into the woman whom God intended me to be. We all need support and guidance in the transformative process of becoming women of God. Choosing to listen to wise and godly women who speak into our lives in a loving manner is an important part of our journey to personal wholeness. We need to be teachable.

It was in 2009, about six months after the "sister friend" meeting, that I realized I was experiencing irritability, fatigue, and lack of creativity. Life was being drained from me as I struggled to juggle my home, career, church, and community activities. I was physically, mentally, and spiritually destitute even though I was actively doing my

Section II: Healing and Restoration

quiet time and serving in my church. Doing the "right things" in the name of God with and for other people does not equal personal wholeness; especially if there is no time to adequately love ourselves.

It wasn't until late in the year of 2011 that I approached more crossroads in life. I was lying in bed after a nap, still totally exhausted. It was as if my entire being became absorbed in the mattress. I thought, "How in the world have I been doing so much all these years?" I was on empty, living on fumes.

Lying in bed I performed a mental inventory of the different areas in my life. I did a self-checkup physically, emotionally, and spiritually. The diagnosis required emergency care. The way I was living was leading to physical, emotional, and spiritual death.

I decided to choose the path to life, which was the road of self-care, not self-sacrifice like I previously thought. Changing my schedule was mandatory. This meant getting rid of anything that was not going to lead to wholeness. I had to say no when I wanted to say yes. You know how it is. You want to serve and be a blessing, and it can feel painful and selfish to say no. But I had to learn to assess what was being asked of me before I automatically said, "yes". I decided, if the "yes" was not going to lead me to my life purpose, then the answer had to be "no". Why? I was using a lot of time and energy participating in activities that were not God's best for me at that time.

We must learn to guard our time and determine what God's best is for us in order to be effective and reach our destiny. People will always seek us out for our gifts and talents, but we must learn when to say no. Trust me, "no" is not a bad word. It is a legitimate word for protecting boundaries.

The next step to wholeness was learning to take better care of my body by making time for myself. I thank God that I was healthy all my life until about 2012, when I was diagnosed with a serious illness. I don't want to go into detail with that story. I have been given a clean bill of health and it is not relevant to my wholeness journey. Previous

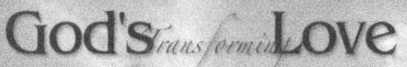

to the diagnosis, I walked several miles a week in the park and tried to limit fast foods, but that was not enough to keep me from getting sick. My schedule was packed as a wife, mother, church leader and career woman. There was no "me" time. I had to learn to set aside time for myself in order to maintain personal wholeness.

Have you ever found yourself promising to start implementing steps toward lifestyle changes only to lay in bed nightly regretting nearly a lifetime of broken promises to yourself? I have. On my journey to wholeness I found myself looking in the mirror every morning at someone tired, with a long to-do list that included me. But the problem was, I never actually got around to checking off the "me items". Items concerning others were checked off at the end of the day. I evaluated the changes I saw in my body from head to toe; wondering when they began and what I could do to regain my youthful beauty. Thankfully, once I implemented and maintained lifestyle changes; I did indeed transform physically, as well as spiritually and emotionally.

Women, remember our bodies are temples of God. Regardless of our shape, size, or skin color we must value being created in God's image. Implementing self-care affords us time to embrace the truth that we have been fearfully and wonderfully made empowering us to unleash true beauty as we journey toward purpose.

Selecting the best route at the crossroads to personal wholeness is the key to balanced living. It is a place that leads to harmony of our spirit, soul, and body. It is the platform of becoming the women God predestined us to become before the foundation of the world (Rom. 8:29, Jer. 1:5) (KJV). There is no question that the Spirit of God has been transforming the souls of believers to become like Christ for generations. Christians don't have to live as scattered or fragmented beings. I have discovered we have a part to play in the transformation to wholeness. We must allow ourselves to become vulnerable to attain harmony in spirit, soul, and body.

In the process of gathering the many fragments of myself, my eyes were opened to how disproportionate my spiritual and physical activ-

Section 11: Healing and Restoration

ities were. I began looking at a scripture differently that is frequently used to emphasize spiritual prosperity in 3 John 1:2 (NKJV) "Beloved, I pray that you may prosper in all things and be in health, just as your soul prospers". The scientist in me began to investigate how to achieve optimal health physically as I pursued emotional and spiritual abundance. God wants our service and worship from a vessel that's whole. You know as well as I do that many Christians ignore health and wellness in the name of serving God. They do not have time for balanced eating, rest, mental health moments, exercise nor keeping routine medical appointments. I am not saying physical health outweighs spiritual or emotional health, but all three must be in harmony in order for us to reach our God-given purpose. How can we share the gospel if we are internally scattered? How can we cast out a life line to those in the margins if you have no strength?

In my profession, which is family medicine, women schedule appointments to request pills to make them feel better. What does better mean? They want a pill to decrease weight, increase energy, increase sleep and even decrease sadness. Unfortunately, pills are not often the sole cure for feeling better physically, emotionally, and spiritually. Statistics show that women spend millions of dollars on beauty products, diets, clothes, education, and reconstructive surgery. Yet, none of those things along mend the fragmented spirit, mind, and body in wholeness. They might temporarily help us feel better about ourselves, but the effect is not lasting. This discontentment can lead to roots that sprout bitterness, depression, anxiety, paranoia, and physical illness.

Often I encourage patients to journal and slow down their pace to get to the root of their problems. Typically, they find the cure in the pages of their journals as insufficient self-care. Sure, medicine has its place in some healing and suffering; however, preventive self-care is always advised. I have found the solution for personal disharmony is to rest in God and applying the practices of lifestyle modification.

Incorporating the following lifestyle modifications into my daily self-care practices has saved my life:

- Applying the scriptures that talk about rest,
- Routine health exams,
- Counseling,
- Saying yes to God's best,
- No to all else,
- Laughing,
- Traveling,
- Spending time with friends and family,
- Making time for recreation and things I find enjoyable,
- Eating healthy, and
- Exercising.*

Yes, I continue to serve in my church, community and work, however, the road to personal wholeness requires me to press toward the mark of a higher calling that includes me caring first for my spirit, soul, and body. Is it always easy to practice self-care? No, but when I can accomplish them without guilt I come alive inside and I feel and look fantastic.

Another component of self-care is caring for our spirits by spending time with God. Many neglect personal quiet times with God, grabbing a moment here and there. One of my favorite scripture verses since college has been Matthew 6:33 (NIV), "But seek first his kingdom and his righteousness, and all these things will be given to you as well". As a student at Fisk University, in Intervarsity Christian Fellowship, I learned how to practice quiet time with God. Some may call it Lectio Divina, devotional time, meditation or a form of contemplative/soaking prayer.

Like Jesus, we must locate a solitary place in the presence of God.

Section 11: Healing and Restoration

"Very early in the morning, while it was still dark, Jesus got up, left the house and went off to a solitary place, where he prayed" (Mark 1:35 NIV). Even in this generation, we need to be cautious not to approach God and studying scripture from a place of striving. Our posture should be from a place of rest knowing that we are the "Beloved" and He has already done the heavy lifting.

Meditative morning time stillness slows us down as it teaches us to stop, look, and listen to our spirit as it communes with the Father. This interaction takes us into a dimension of kingdom living characterized by harmony of spirit, soul, and body. It is in this place of stillness, we find personal harmony and alignment with God to experience contentment.

The Proverbs 31 woman had to be a woman who knew the importance of quiet time. I believe that in the stillness of the morning the Holy Spirit imparted creative strategies to her so that she could effectively lend a hand to her staff, care for her family, and make good business decisions. She was a phenomenal superwoman. As we spend quiet time with God soaking in His presence, He will bless the work of our hands and bring supernatural increase.

I recommend following morning quiet time with exercise, a healthy breakfast, and planning the day. When you make plans for the day, make sure to include moments for mental health like laughter, reading the comics, coloring/painting, listening to music, and times of complete silence. Leave some margins of time in your schedule, because if the day is completely full it becomes difficult to stop and enjoy God's creation. Life is made up of moments, and if we are so busy going from one task to the next we will miss many of those fleeting moments.

Self-care can be included in every moment of your life. Earlier in this crossing I asked a question about your personal self-care. Is your answer the same? Will you continue ignoring the flashing red lights on a path of self-harm to a life of burnout? Will you choose the ancient paths? I invite you to come with me on a life-long journey of transformation by pursuing self-care and rest for our souls. My story is one of learning to live life abundantly as the "Beloved", in pursuit of a life pleasing to the Lord. I pray it will be yours as well.

"A Woman in harmony with her spirit is like a river flowing. She goes where she will without pretense and arrives at her destination prepared to be herself and only herself"   Maya Angelou

***If you want more information about how to implement self-care, visit Trinity Wholeness Ministries' website (trinitywholenessministries.com) for the CD called "Step Out of the Puddle and Into the River of Life."*

Joy Lester Perez is the proud mother of three beautiful adult children and the wife of Hector Perez. Writing, traveling and cooking are her hobbies. She co-authored "Expressions of His Glory" with Lilly Lester; who is her mother. She is currently working on her first solo book entitled "Forgiven, Flawless and Free." She is a member of Faith, Hope and Love Fellowship. Her long term goals are to visit and do mission trips in countries such as Haiti and Africa. She currently lives in Nashville, Tennessee.

My Story, His Glory

Joy Lester Perez

This writing testifies of how God's grace and mercy has covered me. The enemy comes to kill, steal, and destroy our lives, abort our purpose, and divert our will from the will of God, but he is a defeated foe. Due to God's mercy, His unfailing love, His amazing grace, His bowels of compassion, and unmerited favor toward me, I'm still here, and in my right mind, giving God the glory.

At the age of 30, I found myself newly divorced after 10 years of marriage. I was struggling to provide for three children single-handedly, dealing with the stress of the child support system and the stress of just trying to maintain my sanity. I became vulnerable to the enemy, and he tried to take my life and annihilate my

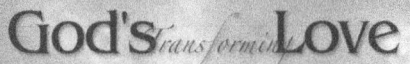

purpose. Just when I thought I could take no more, I had my first Multiple Sclerosis attack.

In May 2006, I was awakened by excruciating pain in my arms and shoulders. Overwhelmed by visual disturbances to the point of being unable to see, and use my limbs. . . nearly paralyzed. I began seeing double, and my equilibrium was affected, which caused my balance to be altered. I put off going to the emergency room because I didn't have insurance at that time. Then I began to have concurrent migraines and burning sensations throughout my body. I stayed in bed all day for two days. My parents insisted I go to the emergency room. I went to the clinic instead, and the doctor ordered me to be taken to the emergency department right away. While in the emergency room an MRI and a CT scan were performed. While waiting on the prognosis, my mom was in the room reading the Scripture aloud. My best friend, Donna, called and prayed with me over the phone from Atlanta, Georgia.

The doctor finally came in, introduced herself, and asked, "Have you ever heard of Multiple Sclerosis?"

"Yes," I replied.

Then she showed me what a normal brain looked like, and then she showed me what my brain looked like. She asked me if I had any questions.

I said, "No."

She said, "You don't have any questions or anything you want to discuss with me?"

I said, "No." Then I thanked her because the whole time in my mind, I was thinking, *I don't receive that!*

The doctor left, and I looked at my mom and said, "I know what the doctor said, and I know what the MRI shows, but I'm going to believe the report of the Lord."

A while later the doctor returned with prescriptions and referred me to a neurologist. I received an expedited appointment with the neurologist, and the months to come were not easy. For the first time

Section II: Healing and Restoration

in my life, I couldn't do anything for my children or myself. I needed help getting out of bed, walking to the restroom, and even just standing up. I was weak and in pain at the same time. My vision was impaired; everything was spinning, blurred, and doubled, which led to me wearing a patch. I was literally bedridden, and my parents had to do everything for me for a season.

I began seeing a neurologist, rheumatologists, and a psychiatrist. My doctor started me on beta serum injections, which were administered four times a week. My doctor forbade me to drive or to work and told me to apply for my disability benefits because I would never be able to work again.

A couple of months passed, and God began to restore my vision and my balance. I was able to take off the patch and resume some of my prior daily activities, but driving was still restricted. The muscle spasms in my arms and shoulders became worse. The burning sensations and the numbness had increased and the pain increased. I was in constant pain. When I walked, my legs would get numb and feel as though they were going to buckle under me.

Multiple Sclerosis is a disease that attacks the nerves in your body. There were times when the nerves felt as if they were breaking through my skin. Other times the pain would start at the top of my shoulder and shoot downward to my fingertips. I've also had an MS attack in both my feet and in my bladder, which affects my body still to this day; but praise be to Jehovah Raphe! I heard and received a word of truth from my pastor, and the Lord restored my vision and balance.

Some symptoms I still experience on a daily basis, like muscle stiffness, nerve pain, and exhaustion. Other symptoms like numbness, burning sensations under my skin and muscle spasms show up often as well. Yet, I still believe I am healed. I don't ever want to forget what God has done for me. I am totally convinced that I am healed from the crown of my head to the soles of my feet continuously.

I shared my diagnosis with you to let you know that God is in control. I decided not to give the enemy any glory for my afflictions.

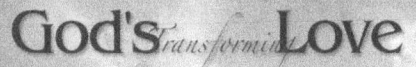

In spite of all the attacks mentally, physically, financially, and emotionally, I'm still here because God has the final say, and He is true to His word and His promises. There were times when it appeared I was down for the count, but my God is a restorer, my healer, my shield, my buckler, my safeguard, my protector, my strong tower, my defender, and the lifter of my head. I'm still standing and will continue to stand because God is the one who holds me up.

The enemy whose job is to steal, kill, and destroy thought after all his tactics and schemes I would be somewhere testifying, "Woe is me!" He didn't realize that I was aware that greater is He who is in me ; and that I would be testifying to the faithfulness, goodness, and unfailing love of my Master. The enemy's plan was aborted, and I am a witness of God's compassionate love and mercy and His unmerited grace toward me. I am redeemed by the blood of the Lamb and the word of my testimony. So I will tell my story and let you know who is responsible for raising me up and healing my body. God can use the most difficult and shameful places of our lives, our stories, for His glory. To God be all the glory!

Dr. Karen Wilkerson is an exceptional teacher, speaker and facilitator. She consults regularly with non-profits creating and streamlining systems. This "administrator extraordinaire" is known for her organizational skills, engaging workshops, seminars, and retreats. She inspires, encourages, mentors and empowers others to achieve their goals and dreams.

Wilkerson earned her Ed. D. in Administration specializing in Organization Development from Kennedy-Western University. She earned a M.S. in Marriage and Family Counseling from the University of Southern Mississippi and a B.A. in Criminal Justice from the University of Southern Mississippi. She is currently working on her Ph. D. in Clinical Pastoral Counseling from Heritage Bible College and Seminary.

Karen sits and has sat on several boards including Gateway Institute, Safe Haven Family Shelter, The Christian Education Advisory Board, and Youth for Christ. She was an active member of Tennessee Business and Professional Women and was Region II District IV Director of the Tennessee Federation 2007-2008 BPW Leadership Team. Karen was voted as Administrator of the year in 2004 and 2005 among the Who's Who of Executives.

Karen is the mother of three wonderful children and lives with her husband of 29 years in Hendersonville, Tennessee.

Trust: It's Just a Journey

Karen Wilkerson

I'm a very private person, and when a crisis hits, my family's response is to immediately close ranks and protect each other. We believe what goes on in our family is dealt with within our family until the situation can be exposed without hurt or harm. Sometimes it's not exposed at all. We don't fight each other, but we fight the enemy.

This makes being this transparent about myself difficult. Exposing myself and trusting God that I am depositing myself in a safe place is new, yet liberating. Not because I'm not grateful for what God has done for me but because I'm moving out of pride and moving into purpose. I moving out of rejection into recovery. I am not ashamed of what God has brought me out of but I look forward to what He's bringing me into. I'm ready to shame the devil, tell the truth, and get my deliverance.

I am a three-year breast cancer survivor. I will be surviving this disease for the rest of my life.

I am writing my story in this collection to bring awareness to a disease that statistics tell us that one out of every eight women in America will be diagnosed with. In 2012, when I was healing from cancer, every 19 seconds somewhere around the world a case of breast cancer was diagnosed among women. In the United States a case of breast cancer was diagnosed every two minutes. Breast cancer is second only to lung cancer deaths among women in the United States.

Many changes happen to our bodies as we grow and mature during our lifetime. Yet, as much knowledge that women may have at their fingertips, many do not know much about their breasts unless they breastfeed or they have a problem. I challenge every woman who reads

Section II: Healing and Restoration

this to educate themselves about the anatomy of their breasts and how they function. This can help you understand which changes are normal and which are not. I won't talk too much more about this because there's so much information out there.

What I do want to talk to you about is *my* story. Someone who is reading this today may find themselves listening to my testimony because what happened to me is nothing new or different. It was how I walked through it that brings glory to our Father.

If I were to use the definition of love I see displayed in the world, my relationship with God would have been conditional at best. It would have been temperamental, impatient, unforgiving and short-lived. It would have been filled with lust with no true feelings attached. It would have been lifeless and one-sided. It would have been all about *me* and selfish, and I wouldn't sacrifice for it. Yet I used this definition and this behavior to define my relationship with God. A God who loves me unconditionally, who is patient and kind, who is longsuffering and forgiving, one who will never leave me nor forsake me. One who sacrificed His Son for me. One who moves Heaven just to be close to me.

When I see love walked out in our world and in the church it sometimes doesn't mirror the kind I read about in the Bible, and I became confused. So when I began battling cancer and going through hell, I tried to draw on that worldly definition of love to pray for a healing and ask an omnipotent God, whom I didn't know how to love, to help me. There is this song by Perry Como, and it talks about catching a falling star and putting it your pocket to save for a rainy day. That's what I did. I caught hold of the Father, the Son, and the Holy Ghost, and I put them in my pocket and saved them for rainy days. Then I wanted to pull them out of my pockets when I was in the midst of something and ask them to perform for me. You see that's not love.

With every fiber in my body, I trust Him. All my life I'd heard people talk about the person they were involved with by saying, "I love him, but I can't trust him" or "I love him, but I can't stand him." How many of you believe that when God saves, He saves to the uttermost? The reason why you can't stand a person is because you don't understand them.

I didn't love myself; therefore, I didn't know how to love God. But God showed me through my six-year journey with breast cancer that my trust in Him meant loving Him unconditionally. Many of you might think, *I do love God.* I love Him too, but now I know how to love and trust Him.

In 2006, I was in my doctor's office all alone when he told me that I had breast cancer and had six months to live. I sat in a room on a cold piece of paper listening to a cold man who knew nothing about me try to pronounce a death sentence on my life. After he told me that, he kept talking, but I didn't hear a word he said. I looked down at my feet and slid off the examination table and tried to catch myself. All I could think of was Scripture and the Scripture verse that came to me was Isaiah 41:10 (NIV): "So do not fear, for I am with you; do not be dismayed, for I am your God." When I straightened myself and stood up, Psalm 118:6 (NIV) came to me: "The LORD is with me; I will not be afraid."

The doctor was steady talking, but I needed more than what he was offering. He was speaking death to me. I then remembered Psalm 118 (NIV): "I will not die but live, and will proclaim what the LORD has done". Now, I had been going to this particular doctor since we moved to this town in 1994, and never before had I seen any Scripture verses in his office. But on that day I looked over on his counter against the wall and saw this verse: "Indeed, he who watches over Israel will neither slumber nor sleep" Psalm 121:4–5 (NIV). The doctor followed my eyes where I was looking, and he said that the nurse had put that in just before I got there, and that he would make sure she removed it.

I mumbled, "No, no, no."

My first response to this news was anger, then fear. I had to catch myself before I said too much and cursed myself or said something

Section 11: Healing and Restoration

that would not represent God. Proverbs 18:21 (NIV) came to me: "The tongue has the power of life and death, and those who love it will eat its fruit." I had to be very careful to guard my life. I gathered my things, got dressed, and went to the car. I sat there and began to pray.

"O Lord, even as I suffer from this thing called cancer, I believe in Your might and Your power. Even as I am besieged by armies of pain, I seek refuge in You. Help me to feel Your presence even more firmly in my life. Give me courage to face anything, to endure everything with You by my side, that I may bless your Holy name through Jesus Christ our Lord. Jeremiah 17:14 (NIV) says, 'Heal me, Lord, and I will be healed; save me and I will be saved, for you are the one I praise.'" What you don't understand about me is that I trust God. I trust He is my refuge, my courage, and my strength. Without Him I am nothing. There is nothing I can't get through without Him. I trust Him that much and more.

As I sat in my car I looked down at my feet and felt that my feet were being fitted with the readiness of the gospel. There was a belt of truth buckled around my waist. I felt the heaviness of the breastplate of righteousness. I dropped my keys on the floor because my arms became weighted down with the shield of faith. I flexed my fingers to grip the sword of the Spirit better. As soon as I felt that helmet of salvation snap into place, I caught myself from losing my mind. I heard a soft voice begin to crescendo in my ear. As it got louder and louder I heard the word "*Fight!*"

I felt the warrior in me awaken. I wasn't going to be a silent lamb anymore. He had equipped me and readied me to fight like I had never fought before.

From 2006 until January 11, 2012, I walked toward God's promise in 3 John 1:2 (NIV) that I may prosper and enjoy good health as my soul prospered. But how many of you know that you have to break down before you get your breakthrough? A compass will point you north, but it doesn't tell you what you will encounter before you get there. My healing was there for me; I had to walk through some things to get to it. Even in that I had to believe the stripes Jesus bore and the blood He shed was for me. Yes, one drop of that blood was for me. My healing was in His stripes because by His stripes I am healed.

During those six years of battling, there were days I couldn't get out of the bed. My hair was shedding. I was losing control of my body. I wanted to cry but wouldn't. I told God I would only cry tears of victory once I was cancer free. But to everyone else it didn't look like anything was wrong. Because I am a private person, it was a jolt to my co-workers when I told them that I had breast cancer and would be taking some time away from work. No one knew. I didn't want people to give me a reason to doubt God. Only my family and a few close friends knew what I was battling.

I found that there are some church people who can be cruel, because some don't know what to say; thus resulting in saying the wrong things. Yes, words, which can hurt very deeply, worse than cancer itself. Sometimes those words can hinder the healing process. There were days when I felt I had thrown up all that was in me, but still my body wanted to rid itself of something, anything. I just sat by the toilet and heaved. There were days when my entire body ached—even my hair hurt and the wind itself hurt. There was nothing anybody could do. Although my husband tried, this was a journey I had to go through in my body alone. I was so weak at times I couldn't think straight, and God knew this was going to happen. Yet every day I got up and went to work and kept functioning and moving. I kept moving north toward God's promise. Because I was grateful. There were people dying from breast cancer, suffering horribly, and literally losing their minds. But I kept trusting God. I thanked God daily for the opportunity to be used. I was grateful that He thought enough of me; He trusted me to handle this assignment.

Every day people asked me, "How are you doing?" Some people looked at me as though they would catch something or as though they

Section II: Healing and Restoration

expected me to just fall apart. But I learned to make confessions when I spoke to people. I used God's promises to keep me anchored. I knew His Word would not return void, so I spoke it with all authority.

After having a bilateral mastectomy and several surgeries in 2012, I was struggling with a whole lot of pain, and my body wasn't like it had been. I knew my life was never going to be the same again. My quality of life would change, and I would have to adapt to the new me. I had carried this disease in my body, incubating it long before it manifested itself in 2006. I was worn out physically and spiritually. I came to the conclusion in December 2012 that I needed to just rest. Catch my breath and rest. This was a different kind of tired for me.

I turned to my husband after my last surgery on December 21, 2012, and I said to him that "I didn't have any more fight left in me." I felt like I wasn't going to be able to hold out for God's promise. Breast cancer had taken away my dignity and femininity. I didn't look like a girl anymore. I didn't feel whole. I would look at myself in the mirror and I wasn't me. I felt artificial and fake. I was smiling and joking on the outside but dying on the inside. No one was hearing my cry for help. There was a crack in my soul, and I was ready to give up.

The very next day on December 22, 2012, with stitches on my stomach and on my chest, I went to work to help prepare for a funeral. My husband decided that he was going with me. He wanted to make sure I did no more than supervise. I went into the building, along with my husband and one other volunteer. I went to the stove and started to light the oven. I lit a match, and the stove went *poof.* It was after my husband grabbed me and kept my blouse from sticking to my chest that I realized I just burned my face, my hair, my arm and my neck. In less than a blink of my eye, 90 percent of my face and 30 percent of my forearm and part of my neck were burned from a backlash of fire from the stove.

I tried to stay as calm as I could, and I began to try to rapidly take charge of my thoughts. Remember life and death is in the tongue. I didn't curse God, but I did get angry. I thought to myself, *I've lost both my breasts; now I am going to lose my face and arm.* With those thoughts, I immediately began to lose my joy. Then pain came in like a typhoon. I was in pain like I had never felt, and I was screaming out to God in the ER, "Please, God, take me." I just wanted the pain to stop, and I thought death was my only option. The ER people had no clue that by cutting away my blouse, they were cutting away some of my stitches, and by pulling on my arms, they were pulling on stitches and damaging my arm.

I really can't tell you exactly what happened or how I got from one hospital to the other. But I do know my daughter was holding my hand when I was screaming, and she anchored me to this earth. My year had begun with such hope and great news. The doctors believed that they had gotten all the cancer; it hadn't spread, and I was cancer free. But now my year ended in dismay, and I was this close to losing my mind. All those Scriptures verses that I drew upon when I heard I had breast cancer vanished from my mind; I had nothing but screams and pain. I was emotionally bankrupt, and I needed God like I never needed Him before.

I woke the next day shattered physically, mentally, and spiritually. I just wanted God to take me during the night, but He didn't. Then I had to do the hardest thing I had ever done. I had to look at myself in the mirror. I lost it. My husband tried his best to encourage me, but he just couldn't. I couldn't halfway see to cry because the skin on my face was so tight. I could barely open my eyes. My right eye was damaged the worst, and there was no sight in it at all. I was broken. I went home, and God allowed me to lay there for a few days not sleeping, not eating, just overwhelmed.

I felt bad for my husband because he didn't know what to do. He had never seen me like this. I had never been like this. He knew I needed support after being devastated and later discharged from the hospital. But, what was the question on his face? God knew . . . there is nothing like support from a true sister-friend.

Section 11: Healing and Restoration

How many of you know there are some true sisters in the church? My neighbor Ms. Gloria came over one day. She kicked off her shoes and went into the kitchen. I heard her talking and being a momma. She took something to the kitchen, and then she came and stood in the doorway of my bedroom. I couldn't see her well, but I knew it was her. I could feel she knew something was wrong, and she paused for just a second. Then she came in and started in on me. She slowly looked at me in my face—the face that was so burned even I couldn't look at it. She began to prophesy to me. I could see God through her eyes, and I began to speak to those things that were trying to bind me. God used Gloria to pull me up out of the pit of hell itself.

"For I was hungry and you gave me something to eat, I was thirsty and you gave me something to drink, I was a stranger and you invited me in, I needed clothes and you clothed me, I was sick and you looked after me, I was in prison and you came to visit me" (Matthew 25:35–36 NIV).

I'm going to end with this: I took some before and after photos of myself. I wish you could see me now. God promised me healing. I had to walk through hell to get it. If you feel like you're catching hell, don't hold on to it. If you're going through hell, don't stop. *What* and *if* are two of the most non-threatening words in the English language. But, if you put them together—What if—they are two words that can haunt you for the rest of your life. They can keep you in bound and gagged. I'm not living in the 'what ifs.' I live in the now. "Now to him who is able to do immeasurably more than all we ask or imagine, according to his power that is at work within us" (Ephesians 3:20 NIV).

I pray daily to God that He continues to restore my joy. On the other side of joy is peace. A peace that passes all understanding. If I told you the whole story of how 2012 almost took out everybody in my immediate family, some of you would wonder how we're still standing, let alone, standing together as a family today. I say I thank God for the opportunity to be used. I'm grateful. I trust that He will restore the years that the locust hath eaten.

God's Transforming Love

    I dare you to trust Him. Put feet to your faith. Rise up and walk toward your healing. All suffering has meaning in God's kingdom. Pain and problems are opportunities to demonstrate your trust in God. Bearing your circumstances bravely—even thanking Him for them—is one of the highest forms of praise. When suffering strikes, remember that God is sovereign, and He can bring good things out of everything. God bless!

Section 11: Healing and Restoration

Courtney Nicole Salters was born and raised in Tupelo, Mississippi and began her relationship with God at her home church, Kimble Chapel Missionary Baptist (KCMB) church. Her parents and grandparents were great examples of God's love and faithfulness and inspired her to develop her own relationship with God. Her understanding of God's character and attributes truly began to flourish in her college years, and her relationship with Him continues to grow.

His life through her has afforded great opportunities and blessings including, but not limited to the following: a beautiful family that loves her unconditionally, a Bachelor of Arts degree from Vanderbilt University (VU), a Master's in Business Administration from Belmont University, a great job working with students at VU, a loving church family at Born Again Church (BAC) in Nashville, TN, and a caring and fun group of friends who are also her prayer partners. She is eternally grateful to God for the great things He has done in her life.

Courtney is excited for the opportunity to share His great love in any way that she can, whether through prayer, singing in worship, counseling, ministering as an Elder at BAC, or writing her story in this book. This God given assignment marks the beginning of her journey as a writer, and she hopes to complete a book that expounds on the subject of food addiction and the abundance of His love and grace.

My Secret Shame

Courtney Salters

How many of us can relate to the excitement that comes with getting ready to eat Thanksgiving dinner at grandma's house? You run down a list of your favorite foods that she is sure to prepare: turkey and dressing, macaroni and cheese, turnip greens, ham on the bone (vastly different from loaf ham), candied yams, sweet potato pie, chocolate cake (or coconut, red velvet, or sock-it-to me, etc.), and peach cobbler. I know your mouth is watering even now. Most of us can appreciate a great home-cooked meal, particularly around the holidays. You can appreciate those times when you plan on being especially indulgent—even "saving up" by eating light before that season of eating, in preparation to go all out. For some of us, this indulgence does not stop at the holidays. It extends into our everyday lives in varying degrees and for a number of different reasons. For many, there is even anxiety that occurs around eating in general, and especially around others, due to how much you might consume and the judgment surrounding that.

You are likely drawn to my story for one of two reasons: out of pure curiosity to see what my secret shame might be or out of utter desperation to be delivered from some shame that you have in your own life. It might be that you, too, are attempting to finally kick a habit or emotional behavior that has plagued your very existence. I can assure you that whether it is smoking or anger or lying or unhealthy eating that has you entangled, you are not alone. We have all been tempted in one way or another to do something we either did not want to or knew we should not do. Sometimes we are able to overcome the temptation with no problem. More times than not, however, we

Section II: Healing and Restoration

succumb to the enticement over and over and over again. I am here to inform you that there is help. There is a power that is much greater than your own willpower to overcome this or that temptation or weakness. It is the power of the Holy Spirit. The source of our only hope for conquering any temptation, weakness, or addiction we might face is God's Spirit living inside us. We have access to complete and total authority over anything that seems to have us bound. Allow me to share with you my story.

For the most part, I grew up as an only child and spent much of my playtime alone with my toys or watching the television. I was extremely studious, introverted, and kept to myself. I was perfectly content to do my own thing without being bothered by anyone else. I remember riding home from school on the bus thinking about getting home to my refuge. I may have had a rough day at school because I was rejected or treated poorly, but I was about to be home. Maybe somebody snickered at me because I looked like I should be in seventh grade instead of fifth due to my height. Perhaps I wasn't included in the group of students who planned on going to the football game that night. Or maybe I was just beating myself up for not speaking up when I thought I should have, instead of just going with the flow. None of that mattered, though, because I was about to be home. There, I would be able to fully be myself and do what I wanted to do. What I wanted to do was eat. I came to realize later that I took comfort in my ability to take control of my happiness by indulging in food. Eating had become a seemingly controllable, yet hopelessly flawed coping mechanism.

It was as though I was trying to fill a need in my life that was not being satisfied. Just like people using a narcotic to escape from whatever present state they found themselves, I was trying to escape. Without even realizing it at the time, I had strategized a way to get away from the pain I felt from rejection or from the emptiness I felt in my heart that made me feel as though I was alone in the world. The interesting thing about loneliness is that it can be felt in the midst of a crowd and even around those who love you. Those side glances from people I thought were judging me because I was an introvert. All the pressure and emotional strain I felt when I couldn't come up with the right words to say at the right time or speak up for myself when needed. It seemed that my personality was inadequate and unacceptable. I felt like an outcast—not "cool" or daring enough to be friends with the extroverts and not the right ethnicity to be fully accepted with the studious. Even while with my family, there were times when I felt like an outcast. My strategy was to pile food on top of the rejection, so I couldn't feel it. The food felt like a great big hug of acceptance.

I have been sort of a "serial snacker" since I can remember—eating one snack or small meal right after the other. I could literally eat six bowls of cereal in a row, without pausing, and this was after eating what most would consider dinner. I have always enjoyed food, but I didn't really recognize it as an issue until my college days and thereafter.

It's interesting how others notice things about you when you move into a new environment away from home or familiar surroundings. My friends would comment, "Courtney, are you eating again?" or "What are you eating now?" Before that time, I hadn't realized I had any sort of issues with food. One other thing I had not considered is the fact that much of my binging took place when I was alone. I would typically eat smaller portions in front of people for two reasons: 1) I knew I would want more food in a short time after that meal, and 2) I didn't want them to witness my binging. In college, it's hard to hide most of your habits because you are around your friends virtually 24/7. You see the good, the bad, and the ugly about each other—including secret addictions.

It didn't seem to be a big deal because I maintained a healthy weight through exercise. I also now recognize that God's grace was keeping me in the way that He fashioned my appetite. I craved mostly healthy foods, which I believe was His way of being there with me. Looking back, I also recognize that overindulging in food or gluttony was my way of compensating for not indulging in what I considered the "bad" sins or the more visible ones. In my mind, since I was a "goody two-shoes," or so I was called, I should have been able to be free in what I ate. Surely, that wasn't a big deal, since I wasn't really overweight.

Then, I tried to stop. At that point, I realized I could not control my binge eating. I was using food to fulfill emotional needs that I didn't even know that I had. It had become such a habit, and even a way of life, that I didn't know how to deal with those emotions without over-indulging.

According to Dictionary.com, the definition of an addiction is the state of being enslaved to a habit or practice, or to something that is psychologically or physically habit-forming, (as narcotics,) to such an extent that its cessation causes severe trauma. It is also simply the condition of being abnormally dependent on some habit.

I came to realize that I had formed a habit of running to food to fulfill emotional needs. Learning about addictions and even about the Overeaters Anonymous organization brought some comfort. Realizing you are not alone in dealing with issues helps greatly in becoming free. I don't really recall going through denial once I realized what was going on, but I definitely recall the utter shame of not being able to stop on my own. To me it sounded ridiculous to be attempting to soothe a craving of loneliness with Frosted Flakes or ice cream sandwiches to forget the fact that you are home alone again on a Friday night (or any night for that matter), or to escape the feeling that your life is not where you had hoped it would be at this point. It was as though I was entering a fantasy world when I was eating. I had control over my own happiness in those times.

When I began to have a true relationship with God, I began to gain an understanding of how He desired that I come to Him to fulfill my needs. He began to show me how my over-indulging was only a temporal fix, and He provided eternal comfort, joy, and peace. In the midst of the pain of not being able to control myself, God revealed to me the power that He had given me by His grace, by the gift of the Holy Spirit, and the manifestation of the fruit of self-control.

Understanding the freedom that God desires us all to walk in made me want to share my story, so others would know they weren't alone. I wanted to be able to share how God is manifesting deliverance in my life by His all sufficient grace and beautiful love for me.

God has given the gift of the Holy Spirit to all who believe in Him and who will receive Jesus as their Lord and Savior. The Holy Spirit, also termed Holy Ghost, is a part of God's triune being or the Trinity, which also includes God and Jesus. When Jesus walked the earth, He was limited by His physical body. He could only provide people with the direct assistance of the Lord if He were actually there with them in His body. When Jesus left the earth in His natural form, He left the Holy Spirit as a comforter, counselor, and helper to live within us (John 14:16, 26 KJV). His victory at Calvary gave us access to the strength of God. We have the very ability and might of the Almighty God living within us to overcome any obstacle.

In order to explain the practical application of this power, we have to understand the details of the Person of the Holy Spirit. Among the varied benefits and aspects of His character is the fruit (divine character) that produces in us and becomes manifest as a result of the Holy Spirit operating in our lives. The fruit is produced gradually as we come to know God more, and it enables us to yield to His will and His way of doing things. Just as an apple tree produces fruit as the tree grows and matures, so we produce the fruit of living a godly lifestyle as we grow and mature in the faith. The entirety of the fruit consists of love, joy, peace, longsuffering, kindness, goodness, faithfulness, gentleness, and temperance or self-control. During this time I learned to practice the fruit of self-control. It is what enabled me to live out God's best for me.

If you are recognizing yourself in my description of being a food addict, then you have likely tried a number of different diets or some sort of food curtailment. One reason these programs don't work on their own is because they can make you self-conscious about your

Section 11: Healing and Restoration

eating habits. If you are self-conscious, then you could become sin conscious and even have a feeling of condemnation and defeat about your ability to overcome the addiction. Any sort of healthy diet program or lifestyle change has to be balanced with the Word of God and completed with the power of the Holy Spirit. Being self-conscious places all the responsibility on your own power to deal with the issue. Instead, God would have you place the responsibility on Jesus and the power of the cross. You have His resurrection power within you to overcome any obstacle as you patiently seek Him. Condemnation is the result of placing faith in your own ability.

Condemnation makes you feel that God does not want to be around you anymore. As a result, you don't pray. You are too embarrassed to read your Bible because you feel as though you broke a commandment or directive from the Lord. If I broke one, I certainly don't want to read up on others I have no power to keep. Condemnation also loves to bring its best friend along with it—shame. What an awful friend to have!

Shame causes you to not only distance yourself from God but also from people. If you are like me, you know it well. The enemy loves for you to feel alone because it makes you vulnerable to his attack. God loves us too much to leave us helpless, hopeless, and alone. The only reason He reveals His law and commands is to show us that we are incapable of accomplishing them without Him (John 15:5 KJV). Romans 8 is full of how He desires us to lean on Him and walk by His all-powerful Spirit to overcome. It is God's grace—His unmerited favor, power, and ability to do His will—that enables us. His grace is sufficient—possessed of unfailing strength—and is ours in abundance (2 Corinthians 12:9; 2 Peter 1:2 KJV).

God's revelation to me about His great love and grace has truly brought freedom to my life. What is so freeing is that I am not on this journey alone. I know that He is with me, and His plan for me is to succeed (Jeremiah 29:11 KJV). It is a daily walk with Him. In the process, I get to know Him better, and I get to know myself better.

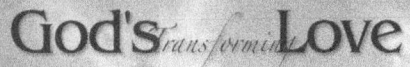

He leads me step-by-step, flooding me with His provision as I yield to Him over my desire for food. I walk out my deliverance from food each day and look to Him when I fall. What's so great about God is that every time I give it to Him, He pulls off another layer of my old self, and brings me to the next level of glory (2 Corinthians 3:18 KJV). I place all my trust in His ability.

Section 11: Healing and Restoration

Ms. Raquel Gammon has always been writing something (poetry, short stories, the next great novel) and is excited to begin sharing her stories with the world. For as long as she can remember, she has always had an idea in her head about a great story, and now has the opportunity to bring those stories to life. Raquel feels very blessed to be surrounded by women who share her same passion for writing. She has been working for over a year, assisting with several writing projects. She is currently working on her own projects, women's inspirational books. Raquel holds a B.A. in Psychology as well as a MBA and currently works in the healthcare industry. She lives in Nashville, TN and is a member of Olive Branch Church.

Grace, Kindness, and Pure Love

Raquel Gammon

I grew up in a family full of love. Although my mother was a single parent because of divorce, she loved endlessly. There was no love missing in my household. It was as if she poured the love into us and filled it to the rim and was always there to fill us up again. My mother was educated, strong-willed, poised, professional, positive, and

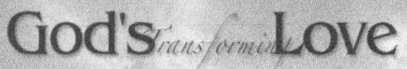

very pretty. She taught me that I had absolutely no obstacles blocking my path and had me believe that I could do anything that I imagined. I watched her work in corporate America and care for my sister and me with the support of my extended family (grandparents, aunts, and uncles) without ever showing signs of struggle.

I can remember several times a year; my mother would dress my sister and me in our best to take us on a dinner date to The Pier. The Pier was a fancy seafood restaurant located on the riverfront in Memphis, TN. I have such fond memories of driving downtown on Riverside Drive, following the line of the Mississippi river toward The Pier. We would watch the river go by as we drove closer to the restaurant, anticipating a fun evening of eating and fellowship. We would speak to the waiter and order our meals like little ladies. We would put our napkins in our laps and eat with our left hands in our laps—just like our poised mother.

My mother made sure that my sister and I had exposure to various experiences for development. She made sure that we attended two weeks of Vacation Bible School every summer, attended plays at the Orpheum Theatre, and participated in charity events to make certain that we were well rounded individuals. We were raised with such grace, kindness, and pure love.

We spent most of our time outside of school in church. We were in church all day on Sunday, from Sunday school, to church service, to dinner in the basement of the church, and quite often an evening program. Wednesday was choir rehearsal, and there was the occasional play, fashion show, auxiliary meeting-rehearsal-performance. We loved every minute of it. Those experiences at Monumental Baptist Church shaped our lives.

From all that my mother poured into me, it was never a question that I would be successful. I always knew that I would be an educated, hard-working, beautiful woman just as my mom so eloquently exemplified before me. And so, I became just that—after great trial.

Section 11: Healing and Restoration

While working on Capitol Hill in Washington, DC, I received the news that my mother had cancer. The aggressive treatment would consist of surgery, then chemotherapy, and followed by radiation. My mother was amazing through the entire treatment, always upbeat and positive and uplifting others throughout the process. She completed the treatment, relieved to be cancer free, and move forward with her life.

One year later, the cancer recurred. It was shocking and very upsetting for everyone close to my mother. She, on the other hand, remained calm and was ready to be as aggressive as before to follow the new treatment plan, which was chemotherapy alone. Soon after my mother was diagnosed with cancer, I was diagnosed with Graves' disease. Graves' disease is an autoimmune disease that affects the thyroid.

I made the decision to leave Washington, DC, and move home to be close to my mom and support her through her second round of treatment. Surprisingly, I would soon find out that I needed her support more than she needed mine. My life had changed so drastically, so quickly. I had just moved from Washington, DC, living on my own and working every day, and then I found myself waking up at my mom's house every day, dealing with a sick body that I had no clue how to maintain. My mom, on the other hand, was popping out of bed every morning heading to the gym to walk five miles.

Each morning this amazing woman would come and wake me and ask if I would be walking with her. I would wake up and respond, "No," and go back to bed. Unlike other illnesses, Graves' disease attacks your mental state as well as your physical state. My body was suffering and so was my mind.

My sister, who had moved from Georgia to be closer to our mom, or I would drive my mother to her appointments for treatments, which she took like a champion. We would all go, just the three of us. We would go to treatment and then find ourselves huddled on the couch watching a movie or watching my niece (a true gift to my mom) do something amazingly delightful.

I started working, and I finally agreed to join the walking club of two with my mom. We walked every morning at 5 a. m. It was very difficult to get out of bed, but it didn't make sense for my mom who was terminally ill with cancer to be so excited about life and living and I couldn't get out of bed. What an example she was for me! I got over myself and walked with my mother every morning; the most difficult part was keeping up with her.

Graves' disease was quickly changing me. I no longer recognized myself in the mirror. There was someone so foreign to me living in my body. This person was very unhappy and very depressed. My life was full of physical pain and mental stress. My long hair was cut short for the third time because my hair had become much like straw; my skin was very dry and ashy-toned, and my eyes had begun to bulge from their sockets.

I can remember walking with mom one morning. I told her I had always been able to lift myself up after a low period, but I was not able to do so at this time in my life. It was a really low point because depression had never been an issue for me. I was always able to lift the mood of others with something encouraging, funny, or just plain silly. I felt a natural ability to do that but could no longer. My mom looked at me with disappointment and explained to me that I had just told her I did not believe in God! I was a bit upset and very embarrassed to realize that I was exhibiting such behavior. I never stopped believing in God; at least that was never my intention. It was then when I was reminded by my mother that God is the source from which all our energy comes. This is why this woman was running circles around me every day while my pain and depression was overcoming me.

I further developed an eye disease attributed to the Graves' disease treatment when I received (radioactive iodine). It is a very rare reaction that I developed. The diagnosis was bilateral proptosis and lid retraction. Bilateral proptosis is the bulging of the eyes due to increased pressure in the tissue behind the eyes, which causes the

Section 11: Healing and Restoration

eyes to bulge out of the sockets as well as eyelid retraction. Eyelid retraction is a result of bulging eyes. The eyelids retract up to compensate for the large bulging eyes, resulting in eyelids that no longer close. I was no longer able to close my eyes, and sleeping with your eyes open is no fun.

My mom was there to support me through this period. I would accompany her to medical appointments, and she would accompany me to mine. We were still walking in our club of two each morning and supporting each other throughout our illnesses. I underwent two surgeries six months apart. The first surgery was the removal of swollen tissue from behind my eyes. The second surgery was to release my eyelids so that they would close again. My mom was with me through each procedure. Shortly after the surgeries, my body was responding to the iodine treatment, and I was slowly becoming me again, although I had a long road to go.

Our walks stopped. I was now bubbling out of bed to find out what my mother felt like doing each day. Most days she just wanted to get ready and prettied up for the day. It was as if my mom saw me becoming myself again and knew that I would be okay. Her health took a turn for the worse, and in a matter of weeks, she was a hospice patient. My mother passed away with my sister and me by her side. She was 56 years old. I will never forget how beautiful and peaceful she was in that passing moment.

After my mom's passing, I had recurring feelings of depression and loss of self that were very difficult to deal with along with my illness. I was living in fear of pursuing my life goals as I once had because of the many obstacles that had been presented in my life. Instead of moving forward and progressing, I existed through each day with no direction for my future.

My sister confronted me, and she told me that it was obvious that I didn't care about anything. She said it would be clear to even those who didn't know me. My darling sister then looked at me and told me that I owed it to God to move from that place of simply existing and to live my life. I realized then that I was living in fear, and I had always been taught that fear does not come from God. I made a decision to trust in God for His promises of plans to prosper me: "'For I know the plans I have for you,' declares the LORD, 'plans to prosper you and not to harm you, plans to give you hope and a future'" (Jeremiah 29:11 NIV). I had been living my life and standing still, and it was time to move from that place of being still and waiting to that place of believing and moving in faith.

As I continued to experience the pains caused by Graves' disease, there was only one way to for me to progress. I held on to my mom's words that God is the source of our energy. I trusted and believed that God would strengthen me each day. I got out of bed and made an effort to live and grow, and that was my prayer. I was very grateful for the blessings of God, and I had no intention for my actions to portray anything different. I made plans for my life and put them on a vision board so that I could see clearly all that I wished to accomplish. I trusted and believed God's Word that I could do all things through Christ, who gives me strength Philippians 4:13 (KJV).

As I look at that vision board today, everything that I envisioned for my life has been accomplished. God has restored my spirit, soul, and body. I may experience challenges, but Graves' disease is no match for the strength that God gives me daily. I live my life in joy every day, knowing that God comforts, protects, and gives me a means to accomplish anything that I can imagine. I know that I have a responsibility to pass this message on to others.

If you allow God to take control in your life, He will show you His Power. You will be amazed at how the Mastermind aligns your life so that you are able to reach those goals that seem so distant.

I am grateful for this opportunity to tell my story because it has

Section 11: Healing and Restoration

forced me to show up for God. I have been hiding from everyone who knew me before my illness. It is very difficult to see the look of disappointment on the faces of those who have not seen me for a while. Those blank stares as if I weren't able to read the writing all over their faces. "What happened to you? Where have you been? I heard you were sick . . . ?"

I once found comfort in hiding and becoming an anonymous person who blends into the crowd unnoticed. That is also a form of fear, and fear will not exist in my life.

I have concrete answers to any question that anyone can ask me about my life. I know that I am a child of God. I know that God loves me as much as He loves any one of His children. And I have experienced the power of God for myself. He didn't heal my mind and my body for me to hide from the world. He healed my mind and my body so that I can show the world what He has done in my life. I will live my life and speak about what God has done for me. I am grateful for the blessings of God, and I will no longer hide.

What I know for sure is that no one receives a perfect life. We all have to deal with something that we would rather not at some time. Whatever it is that you have been given to deal with, how you deal with it determines who you are, and can facilitate your development into a stronger, wiser individual. Life is too short to sit and wait for moments of happiness. We must learn to be grateful for what God has given us and celebrate our gifts at all times. I live every day filled with gratitude and moments of happiness and embrace every experience with grace, kindness, and pure love.

God's Transforming Love

Sonya Little-Jones is a wife, mother, grandmother, and great-grandmother. She serves as a deaconess and secretary of Unity Baptist Church where the pastor is Rev. Harold O. Fields. Her most important role is that of being a daughter to the Master. She proclaims, "He has restored, reshaped, and renewed me." Often, God reminds her of His unending love toward her. She asks, "Who would have thought He would love me enough to give me another chance?" She and her husband reside in Salt Lake City, Utah.

Section II: Healing and Restoration

A Contemporary Woman at the Well

Sonya Little-Jones

MY STORY

Alcohol, tobacco, and drugs; sex, lies, adultery, two families destroyed; a divorced mother of three whose life was spiraling at warp speed toward annihilation; hopeless, helpless, clueless, alone, and lonely. *But God!*

WOMAN OF SAMARIA

The woman of Samaria had been married five times, and the man she was currently living with was not her husband. She was not considered a model citizen. She was shunned; ignored by men; scorned by women; alone; and distraught, making daily trips to the well for water. She went to the well in the heat of the day to avoid other women; she was hopeless, helpless, clueless, and distressed. *But God!*

JUST THE FACTS

Samaritans and Jews chose not to have dealings with one another. So strong was the hatred Jews had for Samaritans that they would walk the long way around to reach Jerusalem rather than take the shorter direct route through Samaria.

Traditionally, men did not talk to women in public, even if it was to their wives. Women who were poor went to the well to draw water; this task was done in the cool of the day, and it was not unusual to find

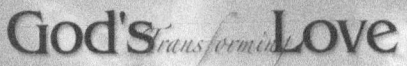

other women at the well at the same time. However, the woman of Samaria (whose name was never revealed in the Scripture) did not go to the well when the other women went. Her daily trip to the well was done in the heat of the day to avoid other people.

Don't think it was a chance occurrence when one day she found herself face-to-face at the well with a Jewish man. This man would change her life forever; this woman had limited knowledge of God but not necessarily with the correct understanding. She was tied to customs, traditions, and explanations passed down from generation to generation; she knew of the promised Messiah but did not know Him. She was hung up on 'where' worship should be done rather than 'who and why.' She had reached a point of despair and was merely going through each day regretting the trips to the well. *But God!*

Jesus was a Jew. He told His disciples that He must go through Samaria in route to Jerusalem, and He came to the well of Jacob. There a little tired and thirsty, He sat down and waited alone. Not long after He was seated came the woman; she was probably surprised to find someone at the well in the heat of the day. She was likely even more surprised when Jesus asked her for a drink from the well. Jesus tore down barriers when He spoke to her and asked for a drink. Imagine her shock when this Jewish man spoke to her in public.

Jesus' actions were an introduction into who He was and what He could do for her. He told her about the Living Water that would quench her thirst forever. She probably wondered, *Could this be true that these daily trips to the well could come to an end?*

Because of her curiosity, she wanted to know more. Jesus told her all her life, from the five husbands to the man she was currently living with not being her husband. He explained to her that He is the promised Messiah. She was so excited with what was revealed to her that she left the well and her water pot and went back to town. When she arrived in town, she told the men about what she had experienced and asked them, "If the man could be the Messiah." The men ran to the

Section 11: Healing and Restoration

well where they talked to Jesus and they were convinced He was the Messiah, and they convinced Him to stay in their town for two days.

Obviously, there are some parts missing from this story, but the important facts are there. You can read her whole story in the Bible in John 4. The important thing is that no matter what condition your life is in or where you find yourself in life, Jesus can change you and your life. He offers forgiveness for sin, hope, help, and unconditional love.

The Samaritan woman's life was changed. She excitedly went into town and told the men of her encounter with Christ, and as a result of her testimony, they all believed and were saved. There is no other mention of her in the Bible so we don't know in what other ways her life was changed. We do know that her life was changed and that transformation resulted in affecting the lives of others.

And so that brings me to my story. I was married at 16 for approximately 10 years. Suddenly, I grew up and started to rebel against my husband and his demands. He didn't know what brought about this sudden change in me, and we butted heads.

Eventually, we got a divorce, and I was alone with our three daughters, trying to figure things out. I thought as long as I worked and provided for my girls, I deserved a good time. I did everything I thought I was grown enough to do. However, there was this void in my life that I could not fix.

The alcohol, tobacco, drugs, sex, and the adultery did not help. At one point, I considered taking the easy way out . . . yes suicide, but I knew that wasn't the answer either. I was alone and lonely. I had no boyfriend; I worked a lot of overtime to make ends meet, so I spent little time with my girls. I thought if I took them out every other week to do what they wanted to do that was sufficient.

One day I decided to make a play for a married man. I thought it was safe because it couldn't be serious, and I could have a boyfriend and my freedom at the same time. *Not so!* The complications started

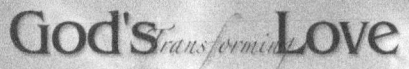

to mount, and eventually my children confronted me about this relationship. I knew it wasn't right. What kind of message was I giving my girls? I didn't want them to think that this was the best they could ever hope for.

I decided to make some changes in my life and called off the relationship. However, that loneliness was too much for me to bear. I couldn't break the bond, so I decided to move back to the home of my childhood. I started going to church and suddenly realized that knowing about Christ was different from knowing Him. Knowing Him meant having an intimate relationship with Him. Who knew it was He who would fill that void in my life? Who knew it was He who would hold me in His arms and tell me everything would be all right? Who knew it was He who would heal my brokenness and tell me that He loves me? Who knew it was He who would change my life forever?

I'm not going to say that everything is peaches and cream, but even in the midst of the storm, He is there with me. He never leaves me, and even when I come up against those strongholds in my life, He is there whispering in my ears, telling me what to do. I have studied His Word, and now I know the promises He offers me. I now know that He loves me, and He loved me even before I knew who He was. His Word tells me that while I was yet a sinner, He died for me. Me the drunk, drugging, adulteress . . . He loves me, and His love has transformed me to be able to love myself and others as He loves me. And if He can change my life and He changed the life of the Samaritan woman, why wouldn't He do the same for you too? He is able to do exceedingly, abundantly more than all we ask of Him. Take His yoke upon you, and learn of Him for His way is easy and His burden is light.

You will find all you need in His Word and in a sincere intimate relationship with Jesus the Christ. He is right there waiting for you to look up from the pigpen of life. He has His arms reaching out to you. Reach out and accept His love and His forgiveness. I promise your life will never be the same no matter what you are faced with from that moment on. He will give you peace, love, and joy like you have never known before. He did this for the Samaritan woman; He did it for me, and He can do it for you too. He restored my family and our relationship to each other. Come to Jesus and be healed.

God bless and keep you.

Personal Life Reflection

When I think of the word *restore*, what comes to my mind?

Why is restoration needed?

In what areas do I need restoration?

What is the formula for restoration?

How have I allowed God's transforming love to restore me?

Section III

Developing and Fighting for Purpose

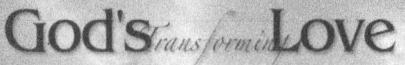

Discovering Purpose Reflection

Lilly Lester

Every human being is born with a definite purpose. Every one of us has a deep need for belonging and expressiveness. However, long before our purpose is revealed to us, Satan begins his assault to abort our purpose by attacking our significance and trying to keep us paralyzed by our past. (praise break) Nevertheless when we come into the knowledge of who God is in us, and who we are in Him, purpose is awakened and ignited into realty. Relationship with God is the first step to discovering purpose. In this section there are 6 stories that display purpose. (The reason for which someone exists or why something is done). You will see aspiration intertwined with purpose and experience God's Transforming Love.

"I raised you up for this very purpose, that I might display my power in you and that my name might be proclaimed in all the earth." (Romans 9:17 NIV)

Section III: Developing and Fighting for Purpose

Lucille Henderson Smith was born and raised in Minden, Louisiana. After completion of high school, she relocated to Los Angeles, California and attended South Western College. Later she pursued a career at the Veteran Administration Hospital, where she was an outstanding employee until she retired almost 31 years later. Early in life, Elder Smith recognized the call of God and began to teach and preach His word. After extensive Bible training, Elder Smith was ordained on October 4th, 2006 in Bluff Arkansas. She is an anointed speaker, teacher, and playwright. Elder Smith is one of God's ambassadors for a time such as this.

Elder Smith presently resides in Memphis, Tennessee. She is fulfilling her passion to "love people to life" and "letting her light shine before men". She has two daughters, one son, seven grandchildren and four great grandchildren.

Lucille can be contacted via e-mail; Ladylulu1942@yahoo.com

A Chosen Vessel

Lucille H. Smith

To everything there is a season, A time for every purpose under heaven (Ecclesiastes 3:1 NKJV)

# God's Transforming Love

There are four seasons in a year: spring, summer, autumn, and winter. Spring is a time of new beginnings. Spring keeps life reproducing and brings forth visions of what God has in store for us. Summer is a time of growth and maturation. The seeds planted during spring mature into full-size plants in the warmth of summer. Summer is a season of diligent works, when we invest our energies and prayers into the crops of life we want to produce.

Autumn is the harvest season. Autumn produces the results of our labor in various stages of life. Autumn teaches us to embrace change in whatever season we find ourselves. Winter is a time of restoration, rest, and reflection. Winter is a time to celebrate and to share life lessons of our faith and gratitude through our journey.

My life journey and story began in the year of 1942. Although born in January, I consider the time of my birth as the season of springtime. It was a very cold Thursday when my mother gave birth to a little girl with bright eyes and a feisty spirit. The baby was named after her sister, Aunt Lucille. I was the eighth child, symbolizing a new beginning, according to the biblical meaning of the number eight. The winter was in full force, cold and rainy. I can imagine my mother's face glowing as if it were actually a beautiful spring day when she cast her eyes upon her new baby girl, making the entire family experience the warmth that flowed from her heart to theirs.

I am sure in light of the lack of resources during this season, this new baby added to the provisional hardship of my parents. However, her joyful response to this new life invoked a sense of new beginnings, renewal of hope in the vision of a better life for the family. My mother was a homemaker with limited skills and my father a farmer. In the mist of her struggles, my mother maintained her inner peace, which gave her comfort in the gift of another baby to nurture, to hold and to call her very own. This new life would love her unconditionally. Her children gave her momentum—a reason to keep going, to endure her hardship . . . just one more day, week, month, and another year . . . one at a time.

Section III: Developing and Fighting for Purpose

During my early childhood, there were challenging moments in which at the age of four my father left the home, and mother continued to demonstrate a strong front for the family. The more I matured, the more I became aware of my likes, and dislikes, trying to find my place among my siblings and peers. For instance, when the other girls and boys my age played in the sandbox or went on hayrides, I didn't participate. This wasn't what I called fun, ending up with sand and hay in my hair and on my clothing. I was a thinker, and often reflected on how and when life for my family would improve.

As I matured I continued to desire a better life for me and my family, perhaps even appearing aggressive, and an overachiever. Basically, unable to verbally communicate my faith, a result of a seed planted by my mother, I knew God had a good plan for us. I was in search of purpose and strategies to escape the generational struggles I now know plagued my family.

It is clear now I was in pursuit of change for a better life. Every day was important to me at home, school, and playtime. Each daily activity I participated in had to have meaning to my journey toward purpose. In some ways I was an overachiever. For instance, I was the first one in my class to learn to read, and I excelled in math. I sought the teacher's approval in class and in homework. I enjoyed the fine arts, especially drama, and was often the lead in many school plays. It was as though a force was driving me unbeknownst to those around me, like the presence of a human guide or coach.

I am sure my teachers had an impact on me, but I was self-motivated. I felt compelled and chosen to find a solution for my mother. This is why Jeremiah 1:5 (NKJV) resonates with me as it says, "Before I formed you in the womb I knew you; Before you were born I sanctified you; I ordained you a prophet to the nations." I felt I was chosen.

There were family members outside the home who wanted to raise my baby brother and me, but intuitively I knew it was better to remain connected with my immediate family. It's like deep down inside I knew that change was coming–a new season. In retrospect, I realize I was chosen to be raised by my mother for this journey. I am a living testimony that Psalm 37:25–26 (NKJV) is true: "I have been young, and *now* am old; Yet I have not seen the righteous forsaken, Nor his descendants begging bread. *He is* ever merciful, and lends; And his descendants *are* blessed."

Over the years, I grew in wisdom and knowledge of my purpose in life, learning that in time there is a reason for each season. Just as the Scripture says, "To everything there is a season, A time for every purpose under heaven" (Ecclesiastes 3:1 NKJV). As we fast forward from junior high and high school to graduating as number thirteen in the class and being inducted into a National Honor Society, I planned to launch out into the unknown… a new life. There were many painful experiences waiting for me after graduation. Three days later, I left my small home town, Minden, Louisiana, and headed for the bright lights of Los Angeles, California. This is where I was able to take a peek at who I was and why I was. My great awakening was about to start and continued for many years. It helped me to realize how precious the life values were that had been instilled in me by those who loved me. These values sustained me.

In the 1960s, I served as a minister of music and bible teacher at True Vine C.O.G.I.C for the youth ministry for several years. As time progressed with family and friends who were migrating to the great nightlife of Los Angeles, I found myself being lured to the ballroom floors. I even tried to fit in with the party group that did the nightlife in style. I look back and laugh about the times I tried to drink but didn't know how to drink or what a lady should order to drink. I ended up ordering the stronger drinks that were for those who were more experienced. I would even out-dance the other dancers, trying too hard to fit in. I can now praise God for watching over His investment in me. I got very close to the edge, but didn't go over the cliff. God's hands were on His chosen vessel.

In the meantime, I was blessed to be employed by the government

Section III: Developing and Fighting for Purpose

at the Veterans Administration hospital in West Los Angeles in March of 1965. According to the news and what I was able to observe, the city was in turmoil. It was during the Watts riots when I was employed as a psyche tech, caring for the well-being of veterans. I came every day during this tumultuous time to support the hospital. Once the city was able to adjust to this upheaval and return to some normalcy, I received an honorary commendation for loyalty to the patients and staff during the riots. It was at the VA hospital where I met Carl Smith, my soul mate, whom I married. I later became the mother of three children—two daughters and one son. During this time I went to college, worked, and began serving again in church as a dedicated wife and mother. In this time of life my faith grew, and I accepted my call into the ministry as an evangelist. I began to diligently seek God's direction for my life. I enrolled in the C.H. Mason Bible Institute for two years, along with my husband.

Little did I know that my life was going to be filled with seasons of much suffering that would reveal God's purpose for my life. Challenges began to occur in our lives in succession: sickness, accidents, finances, and personal health challenges of my own. I continued to ask myself why there was so much suffering. The answer never came. We just did what we could, hoping it would soon pass. As I moved deeper into my summer season, some of the struggles disappeared, especially the financial ones. Our family was able to take month-long vacations, visiting family members in other states. My son often referred to our family as the true Huxtable household modeled after *The Cosby Show*.

A major change took place in my life July 21, 1992. While I was preaching a revival in Los Angeles, my husband died. I was in the fifth decade of my life and I decided it was my end. It was a very difficult time for the family, but through it all I learned to put my trust and hope in the Creator of this vast universe.

In 2003, while experiencing medical issues with my heart, I was asked this question by the Holy Spirit: "Why die before your winter ends?" And immediately the seasons for my life were revealed to me: the spring time is from birth (0–30), summer (30–60), autumn (60–90), and winter (90–120) years. This is not the end, it is where I realized I was in late summer, entering autumn.

It was there in the big city that I comprehended that God had great plans for my life, and I was to be a chosen vessel. Jeremiah 1:5 (NKJV) became alive to me in the summer season of my life. I reentered Bible college. I was also blessed to learn from the teachings of one of God's great generals: Bishop J. O. Patterson Sr. of C.O.G.I.C. I was ordained as an elder and evangelist in the C.O.G.I.C.

A few responsibilities of mine were teaching Sunday school for a number of years at the Cook Convention Center during the C.O.G.I.C National Convocations in Memphis, Tennessee. I have been blessed to serve as a teacher of the word while living in California and other states.

In late summer around the year of 1998, on March 3, I retired after working 30 ½ years for the Veteran's Administration, the VA in West Los Angeles, Long Beach, California and the VA in Memphis, Tennessee. I was honored by the director for outstanding service at the VA in West Los Angeles.

The joy of having ministered to the veterans can't be described in mere words. Providing care for mental wholeness in group sessions, a listening ear, and other occupational activities to assist with the comfort of their Post-Traumatic Stress Disorder (PTSD) were just a few of the tasks I was sent to do. My work gave me the inner feeling of peace that I experienced after doing what I was called to do with the spirit of excellence. Praise God for the many years of being a chosen vessel and having a listening ear to hear the veterans' spoken and unspoken concerns.

After my retirement, the book *Mother Behold My Sons* was birthed and is to be published soon. It was the first of many writings the Spirit of the Lord has given me to bring hope and healing

Section III: Developing and Fighting for Purpose

to the masses for His glory. Full-time ministry of teaching God's Word and ministering to the hurting is my passion as a chosen vessel.

Presently, in my autumn season, I am happy to testify my heart is fixed and my mind is made up to be an instrument used by God for His glory at all times with gladness and without regrets. I am God's chosen vessel. I am a woman, but my life's suffering is similar to Apostle Paul's, who was also chosen. Acts 9:15–16 (NKJV) says, "But the Lord said to him, "Go, for he is a chosen vessel of Mine to bear My name before Gentiles, kings, and the children of Israel. For I will show him how many things he must suffer for My name's sake.""

In your time of doubt, discouragement, and hopelessness, remember you were chosen before the foundation of the world. God has a plan for you and a future not to harm you. Keep Jeremiah 29:11 (NKJV) before your eyes: "For I know the thoughts that I think toward you, says the Lord, thoughts of peace and not of evil, to give you a future and a hope." Hold up your head, and prayerfully seek God for direction to fulfill your purpose.

God's Transforming Love

Crystal Martin grew up in Cerritos, California. She decided to stay in the south after graduating from Western Kentucky University. She is a faithful member of Born Again Church and Christian Outreach Ministries in Nashville, TN. Crystal is the director for an organization that manages the aging. She presently resides in Smyrna, Tennessee. She has a son, and daughter. She loves to travel, and help people get true freedom in their finances.

After The Divorce, Out of The Pit

Crystal Martin

Sometimes in your life it seems you were dealt nothing but lemons; however, the funny thing in life is that most of us don't understand that God turns those lemons into lemonade. When I decided to get married, I was looking for a provider, and I had a fear of getting older because most people I grew up with were getting married. My way of thinking was that women finish school, get married, and live happily ever after. I knew marriage would be work, but I thought because my husband was saved, it would solve every problem. However, it couldn't because

Section III: Developing and Fighting for Purpose

we both wanted different things. I was young, and I didn't know how to allow God to help me grow in the process. I felt like my whole life was a barrel of lemons. Although I was married, I constantly felt alone. I felt like I was drowning in a pit of despair and I couldn't climb out of it. I couldn't seem to find the help I needed to get through this time. Eventually, my marriage ended in divorce.

To look at me, it appeared that all was well, but when I was alone, my emotions hit me like a ton of bricks. An inner voice kept reminding me about being alone, rejected, and that I was a failure. I thought, *"God, You love me, so why is this happening to me?"* I just couldn't see the upside to anything in life. The pain had caused me to become hard, even though I fought against it. Life became routine as I struggled to take care of my two children and myself. I didn't trust people or their intentions because my friends who were married removed themselves, especially when I needed their support.

I understand now they just didn't know how to help me. But a very wise person told me, "In order for something good to go in, the bad has to be talked out." I felt at that point that I needed someone to listen. I realized that I must seek counseling. As I heard other people's plights, counseling helped me tear down barriers of my heart and allowed me to trust and live again one day at a time.

How quickly God can turn a situation around, whether He uses scripture, a personal encounter, a person, or a song. For me it was a song. I was driving down the road one day, and I was singing a song, "We've Only Just Begun," by Karen Carpenter.

I was broke. I was raising my kids alone, so how was my life going to become great? But God already had the answers and the plan. A few weeks later, I went with my friend Lisa to a Joyce Meyer conference in Nashville. I told the Lord that day that I was in deep need of help and to please give me a word.

Joyce Meyer walked out on the platform, and she said, "I don't ever do this, but the Lord said there are a handful of women whose husbands have just recently left them." She was very stern in that she didn't want everyone near the platform, just the women whose husbands had recently left. I ran down there because I knew she had a word from God. I assumed she was just going to pray over all of us at the same time, but she prayed individually for me. There were approximately 13 ladies at the front. She said, "God wanted me to tell you He has a plan for your life, and He will fulfill it in you." I was so excited. *God, You really do love me.*

God can turn a situation around so fast that you don't remember much of the pain or things that you went through. Forgiveness is a major process of choosing to forgive on a daily basis. Sometimes the person will come back and tell you he or she is sorry for what happened, but sometimes it doesn't happen that way. In my Christian walk, I learned that I have to image the cross and nail the issue there. However, today my ex-husband and I are on friendly terms. I love to see him when I get a chance. He is a good person inside. I don't remember that old person I was married to. I walk in total deliverance.

God was doing something in me, in allowing me to understand that life is not always perfect. Now I have learned that in the process of forgiving someone I have to look at his or her past or what he or she might be going through. You find God's mercy for that person. People who have hurt you may have been abused as a child, sexually or physically. They could have been rejected or had abandonment issues. Whatever the case may be, once you step outside of yourself, you see that person's behaviors that hurt you might have occurred due to past issues. All you can do is pray for their deliverance.

My miracle is that I don't remember any of the pain while in the marriage, nor do I remember how angry I was during my divorce. I have had many things happen to me in my life, and the enemy could have used this as a way to keep me in bondage. However, trust me when I say that for whatever reason, God knew I could survive this too. I will say in this journey that I have learned it takes two people to make or break a marriage. Sometimes we forget to keep God at the center.

Section III: Developing and Fighting for Purpose

Sherry Jackson is one of 10 children who moved from Gary, Indiana to Nashville TN in 1984. She later attended Business College and graduated in 1988. She is a single stay at home mom/caregiver of 4 children, 3 of which are Autistic. Sherry is a member of Born Again Church where she has served on the usher board ministry for many years. One of her hobbies is Horticulture. She is presently working on her book, "Raising 3 Autistic Children, yet standing and praising God."

Not Forgotten

Sherry Jackson

I am blessed to have been entrusted with four beautiful and precious children, three of whom are autistic. My daughter Ariel is now 25 years of age and continues to blossom into a charming young lady. My twin sons, Weslie and Leslie, are 21 years of age. They are both handsome and loveable. Brittany, my oldest daughter, is a graduate of Vanderbilt University. She also received a master's degree from Lipscomb University. I am so very proud of her. Her love for her siblings and me has kept us afloat many, many times.

In my darkest days, I thought my only answer was suicide. I felt that life for me was hopeless. It felt like God was punishing me and had forgotten about me and my children. I had planned to take Weslie

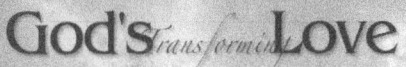

with me because no one would understand or love him the way I do, but God intervened and told me, "Absolutely not." This is not what He created me for, and He had another plan for my life. I just had to believe that God thought I was pretty special to bless me with the care of these beautiful angels, my children. God is love, and that is what I see when I look into the eyes of my babies: total unconditional love.

Although we have experienced really difficult times, we have also had many wonderful times. Most recently, we shared in Brittany's beautiful wedding. Ariel was a bridesmaid, and Weslie and Leslie were groomsmen. It was an unforgettable day of love and memories.

During the period of darkness, depression became my best friend, but I believe God heard my prayers and bottled every tear, even when I closed myself off from the world. My world was my children and me. I wouldn't answer phone calls or open the doors. I must admit, however, my family and other people did try to reach out to me, but I would always think, *how can they understand*? They have not walked in my shoes. Our family survived on the children's Supplemental Social Security Income, along with sporadic child support and with the generosity of friends. We got by because of the sheer grace of God.

A few years ago, Weslie, who functions at a 16– 36-month-old level, climbed atop a television stand to reach for a picture on the wall. His doing this caused the television to fall on him and shatter his left leg. Before he recovered, he jumped off our apartment balcony, breaking his right ankle. The Autism Society of Middle Tennessee put Weslie's story on their website with my permission. During one typical busy day, I had no time to answer the phone again, but God said, "You're not too busy today." So I answered the phone, and on the other end of the phone, there was the sweetest, soft voice of a lady introducing herself and asking me if she could be of any help to me and my kids financially. She then told me how she had gotten my phone number and how she knew of my situation. By that point, I was in complete shock. My ears, eyes, and

Section III: Developing and Fighting for Purpose

mouth were wide open. My first thought was, "God has not forgotten me." He had sent His angels my way.

She then shared with me that she too had three autistic children, two boys and a girl. I was totally knocked off my feet. Two of her children were twins. By then my heart pounded wildly, and my chest felt like it was going to burst. Tears welled up in my eyes, and I knew for sure that my God had not forgotten me and that He loved me with all my faults and mistakes.

She then asked me for a favor after a long morning conversation, "Could I please call you from time to time?"

I shouted, "Absolutely!"

She said to me, "You have gotten this far raising your children alone, and I have a husband and family. If you can do it, I know I can do it. You are a very strong woman."

I began to thank her, but I did not feel strong at all. When we got off the phone, there were tears, tears, and more tears. I kept thinking that only God could have brought someone in my life with the exact situation to reach out and touch me when I had so carefully made sure no one would get in.

After this encounter, this woman and many others reached out to me offering help in any way they could: washing, cooking, shopping, and financial aid. It seemed like nothing was too much for them to help me in my overwhelming time of need.

I finally realized depression, doubt, and fear had paralyzed me and caused me to become a recluse, which resulted in shutting out family, friends, and even God. Praise God that He wouldn't let me go! Just at His set time, every wall that I had tried to build was slowly coming down.

As the days, months, and years passed, I was still the single mother with three autistic children, still asking God, "Why me, Lord?" I never smoked, drank, or did drugs, yet my children as well as I were

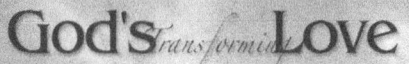

being punished. As I began to seek God for answers concerning my family, I remembered that I had accepted Christ at a young age, and as a young adult, I had strayed away from Him. However, I knew in my heart, He had never left me. He waited lovingly and patiently on me to return. He knew He had work for me to do through my obedience that would bring glory to Him. Oh, how I praise Him for His grace, mercy, and His steadfast love for me. My situation did not change, but I had changed. My struggle ended when I became fully aware of how much God loved me and that He had already paid the price for everything my children and I would ever need.

God's amazing love, the sacrifice of His Son, and His Holy Spirit sustains me moment by moment, day by day, week by week, month by month, and year by year until Jesus returns.

Section III: Developing and Fighting for Purpose

Tonia Scott was born and raised in Nashville, Tennessee. She is currently working as an information technology security account administrator. She is also a licensed cosmetologist and as an independent consultant. She served on the Nashville State Community College Board and was a director of a Christian school's after-school care program.

She enjoys spending time with her family and being a wife and mother. She rises early to prepare her home to be a home of peace and prayer. One of her favorite Scripture verses is from Proverbs 3:5–7 (NKJV): "Trust in the LORD with all your heart, And lean not on your own understanding; In all your ways acknowledge Him, And He shall direct your paths". Her hobbies are cooking, hosting guest in her home, scrapbooking, sewing, skating, and helping others. She is an advocate for youth and children. Her *life speaks* as a motivational speaker.

Our Life Speaks

Tonia Scott

My life resembles the formation of a diamond. It consists of characteristics that embrace my expression as a woman, wife, mother, sister, and friend. People are attracted to diamonds because of their brilliance, just like people are attracted to one another often because of their exterior and not always because of a reflection of their interiors.

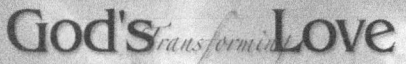

God's Transforming Love

My story is one that teaches the reader to understand that rough places are a process of the passages of rite that will strengthen and develop character. It's important to understand people are like diamonds; they are unique. Similarly, to people, diamonds have characteristics that determine their value.

Gemologists have identified what they call the 4Cs. The Geological Institute of America (GIA) is one of the largest, most respected non-profit sources of gemological knowledge in the world. The 4Cs represent clarity, color, cut, and carat. These attributes determine diamonds' beauty and obscured blemishes as they sparkle at us from the showcase.

On my journey, my life bears a resemblance to the 4Cs. The diamond's characteristic clarity is the result of carbon being exposed to tremendous heat and pressure. This process can result with a variety of internal characteristics called inclusions and external characteristics called blemishes.

Retrospectively, I can see how my life parallels with the formation of the diamond and my formative years of who God predestined me to become. My mom and dad were barely teenagers when they got married. I was told that their marriage was pre-arranged. Who knew blacks had pre-arranged marriages? When I learned more about their marriage, I realized it wasn't exactly pre-arranged. Their marriage was the proper or less shameful thing to do since my mom was fourteen and pregnant, and my dad was eighteen years old. My sister was conceived first and then another child, and finally followed by me. It was tumultuous times for our family, and divorce was being contemplated.

I remember playing over and over in my head mother's voice saying: "I was just too young to be married and now trying to raise three kids with an unfaithful husband." I also remember her saying: "Our parents made us get married. They were not going to be put to *shame*." Many years of internalizing those words passed, wondering if my existence was something they were proud of or was I a blemish of their

Section III: Developing and Fighting for Purpose

mistake. The stigma of possibly being unwanted persisted in my mind as I developed into a young girl.

"Before I formed you in the womb I knew you, before you were born I set you apart; I appointed you as a prophet to the nations" (Jeremiah 1:5 NIV). This scripture verse resonated loudly in my heart, confirming my being unique and set apart even before I was formed in my mother's womb to help give me clarity to my existence.

It was after my parents' divorce when my siblings and I witnessed some pretty dark days. We were sometimes separated from each other and constantly back and forth between the two parental home environments. It was not until I reached the age of 12 when there was any stability; finally, we were permanently with my dad until adulthood.

When I was 18, I formed an opinion about my life and about my parents. I decided I would not make the same mistakes my parents made in terms of relationships and parenting. I would not drop out of high school, and I would go to college. I would not be a part of the statistics by having my children before marriage. I wanted *no* part of that!

How was I to accomplish this with the dysfunctional examples I witnessed and the multi-residential environments that encircled me? The development of my foundational years were really unclear, including my ideas and opinions. I did not realize then that my parents, like myself, were as clueless as they were because they were products of their situation. They were immature with adult issues. The cloudiness of their self-identities impacted my identity.

In order to give clarity, let's look at the 4Cs and how they help explain my story. The color of a diamond represents its quality; The quality is based on the absence of color. The clearer the diamond the better its quality. A chemically pure and structurally perfect diamond has no hue, like a rain drop of pure water. Imagine that: nothing was really black or white for me, just shades of gray, and sometimes life was totally empty of any color. After a lot of trial and error, choices added blemishes to my life.

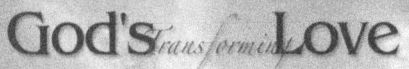

A lot of the choices I made were through the window shades of my childhood rearing, including the ones that soothed the internal hurts. I tried to be better and better and took a mid-stream detour. I said, "I'm going to do what my parents did not do." But somehow I found myself doing exactly what they were doing, making childlike decisions. There were some situations escaped but not all of them.

My son was conceived when I was 24—10 years older than when my mother had her first child. Was history making a circle? No, I wasn't married to my child's father, and believe it or not, I almost repeated the act of marrying his father because of the pregnancy out of wedlock, but I did not. I chose the forbidden shame! I was determined to take the other road.

I took a detour in my life as I searched for a truth. I remember the detour so vividly that it seemed like just yesterday. I began to hunger for *truth*, an *absolute*! In searching, I surrendered with a contrite heart and a messed-up head and impaired vision, and I asked God to help me.

It wasn't until I surrendered my life to God that He began to impart this truth: that I was predestined and not a mistake on the part of my parent's choices. When I totally surrendered my life, He separated me from a lot of superficial thoughts and anything that would sway me to believe less than what He had predestined. That's when my thoughts became clearer—not so gray—but colorless (pure). He called me a diamond, and I heard "a diamond in the rough but a diamond sho'nough!"

"I will sprinkle clean water on you, and you will be clean; I will cleanse you from all your impurities and from all your idols" (Ezekiel 36:25 NIV). Our lives speak when the Lord comes into our hearts and shows us what we were created to be and how He made us in His image and likeness, peeling away the layers of life that was added during the process of coming to this world. Our lives speak when the diamonds in the rough and the process of being refined and defined from the environments or elements of life's storms polish and shape us.

The third C refers to the cut of the diamonds. A diamond's cut unleashes its light! Diamonds are known for their ability to transmit

Section III: Developing and Fighting for Purpose

light and sparkle intensely. A diamond's cut is really about how well a diamond's facets interact with the light. Precise artistry and workmanship are required to fashion a stone so its proportions, symmetry, and polish deliver the magnificent return of light only possible in a diamond. A diamond's cut is crucial to the stone's final beauty and value. This passage in Scripture refers to the light of Christ shining through you as you are enlightened with the truth: "Everything was created through him; nothing—not one thing!— came into being without him. What came into existence was Life, and the Life was Light to live by. The Life-Light blazed out of the darkness; the darkness couldn't put it out," John 1:3–5. (THE MESSAGE).

The fourth C refers to a diamond's carat. The carat of a diamond measures the weight of the gem. Similarly, the trials that I have endured describe the weight of who I am in Christ, and that is immeasurable. My life speaks now with renewed vision and with a hope for the next generation. The task of breaking generational curses is obvious to me. Under pressure of life, I chose God's redeeming love to create a legacy of love as God has shown me that He prepared for me.

Even when suffering for being a Christian, the following verse departs this truth: "Dear friends, do not be surprised at the fiery ordeal that has come on you to test you, as though something strange were happening to you. But rejoice inasmuch as you participate in the sufferings of Christ, so that you may be overjoyed when his glory is revealed. If you are insulted because of the name of Christ, you are blessed, for the Spirit of glory and of God rests on you. If you suffer, it should not be as a murderer or thief or any other kind of criminal, or even as a meddler. However, if you suffer as a Christian, do not be ashamed, but praise God that you bear that name" (1 Peter 4:12–16 NIV).

You might ask how your life speaks. My life speaks to others when I trust God. He shows me who I am in Him, and He shows me the many different facets of His light that speak from the life I've been given and the life I am living. Much like a diamond that has facets of

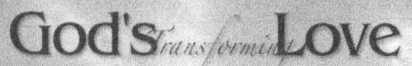

light that are displayed from it, depending which way the light hits it or whichever way it is turned, there is a purpose for it. It really doesn't matter how I got here or how different I am, but one thing is for sure: I am God's plan and so are you. You are predestined for greatness, full of purpose, and full of God's light!

Today my life speaks volumes to those who dare to watch how Christ—through mentorship, the scripture, and prayer—refined and polished me. I had many doubts early in life, and I thought I would become a statistic. But I have chosen to sparkle for His glory as His molding hand has transformed me. What will you do with your life?

God helps us to do what we can,

And endure what we must,

Even in the darkest hours,

But more, He wants to teach us

That there are no rainbows without

Storm clouds and there

Are no diamonds without heavy

Pressure and enormous heat.

-Author Unknown

Section III: Developing and Fighting for Purpose

Denotra Sharpe Sneed is a dedicated K-4th grade teacher at the Bethlehem Center of Nashville. Music is an integral part Denotra's life. She is known for sharing her gift throughout the body of Christ and with other Christian artists. She is a Praise and Worship Leader at Born Again Church in Nashville, Tennessee, ushering people into the presence of God. Her forthcoming single, *Denotra,* is soon to be released. Denotra's ministry of praise and worship brings healing and revives the soul and spirit. Denotra lives in Nashville, Tennessee and is married to Charles Sneed.

Contact Information: charlesanddenotra@gmail.com or charlessneed@gmail.com

This Is My Story; This Is My Song

Denotra Sneed

My story begins when I came into this world with complications at birth. I was told I came out feet first, which is called a breech birth, and on top of that, my right lung collapsed. So the doctors told my mother, father, and the rest of the family that the doctors would have to do immediate surgery on my right lung. But God already had a plan for my life.

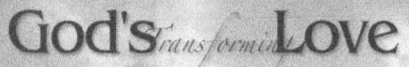
God's Transforming Love

From my earliest years, I have had a love for music that allowed me to bury my insecurities and feelings that were rooted due to shyness and weight issues. My mother and grandmother noticed that I loved music and loved to sing. I would always have the radio on, sitting on the floor and singing the songs. I remember asking my mother if she would buy me a tape recorder so I could tape the songs off the radio that I liked. I wanted to play them back and learn how to sing them. She did, and I was so happy. Even then I would have my private concerts long before I started singing before people.

Little did I know that through my grandmother's teachings about God, and watching her impact so many young people, that God was preparing me for a music ministry. At age fifteen, I began to sing around the city. I was a very shy, overweight teenager, longing to be accepted by my peers, which lead to unhealthy relationships. My mother and grandmother prayed for me through this difficult time. I can remember this was the beginning of a long, lonely season.

My later teens and young adult years were filled with frustrations and disappointments. I was always waiting for something good to happen for me. But God would always show up and remind me that I was not forgotten. God began to open doors of opportunities for me to sing locally while I was learning how to cope with my insecurities. Later when I learned to pray and meditate on His Word, God let me know that He had a plan for me. I found the scripture on God's plan in Jeremiah 29:11(KJV), "For I know the thoughts that I think toward you, saith the Lord, thoughts of peace, and not of evil, to give you an expected end."

My problems did not disappear overnight, but God began to teach me how to trust and wait on Him. I began working on myself by facing my giants. This was the beginning of a total makeover for me. As I put my petitions before the Lord, He showed me that really I was not forgotten. The things that kept me in a state of frustration primarily were my weight and fear, but I had a new focus on God and His will

Section III: Developing and Fighting for Purpose

for my life, and I wanted to be filled with His Spirit. I wanted more from God in my season of singleness, but there was much loneliness and emptiness, which caused distractions in my walk with the Lord. I wanted to be loved and accepted by my male friends, but I was disappointed. But God in His faithfulness began to open doors of opportunities to the gifts that He had blessed me with to use for His glory. I began to travel and sing not only locally but also abroad. My life centered on singing.

Just when I thought my life was about to take off, I remember waking up and preparing for work one day. When I looked into the mirror, I was surprised so see my face was twisted. I took another look to be sure of what I'd seen. Tears begin to roll down my face uncontrollably. My first thought was that I must have had a stroke.

I was in pain, but I pressed my way to work. One of my co-workers took me to the hospital, and the doctors ran different tests on me. The diagnosis was Bell's palsy, which is a temporary facial paralysis, resulting from damage or trauma to the facial nerve that can derive from high blood pressure, flu-like illnesses, diabetes, or stress, just to name a few of the symptoms.

With God's help, I went to work and church faithfully, and gave 100 percent, even in my pain and shame. I stood in my place still leading worship and gave God my all, although I couldn't smile, but believing and standing on God's Word for my healing. Romans 8:28 (KJV) became my confession: "And we know that all things work together for good to them that love God, to them who are the called according to his purpose".

However, this was a very hard place for me emotionally. There were still two things I never gave up on: my music career and my dream of being married. Four years later, the Lord blessed me to marry my best friend of 13 years, all the while healing me physically, emotionally, and spiritually, that I might continue to do the work of the Lord. I have been married to my prince for 12 years.

God's Transforming Love

To my sisters who are still trusting and believing for a mate, or a dream to manifest, or you find yourself in transition, God has not forgotten you. Continue to delight yourself in the Lord, and He will give you the desires of your heart (Psalm 37:4 KJV). I found it to be true when I learned to delight myself in the Lord; my desire became to know His heart even the more. I am still learning how to prevail over my challenges, even today, and to trust in the Lord with all of my heart. I would encourage everyone who reads my story to follow Psalm 37:4 (KJV). Receive it, believe it, and live it, and it will change your life. Challenges will come and go, but God is greater!

Today I stand as a strong mature woman in God. I am ministering as He leads, conducting praise and worship workshops and leading worship for churches and conferences. I am a recording artist, mentoring young girls and young men, and I am actively involved in local women's ministries.

I want to let you know that no matter the stress, frustrations, hurts, disappointments, loneliness, fear, loss of a love one, or even the strain on your finances—and the list of trials and challenges can go on and on—I know that it took prayer, faith, and worshiping God to make it through! We know that our trials come to make us strong, and just like me, one day you will have a song. I leave you with the chorus of this song, "Blessed Assurance," which has sustained me.

This is my story, this is my song,
Praising my Savior, all the day long;
This is my story, this is my song,
Praising my Savior, all the day long.

Blessed Assurance by Frances J. Crosby, *1873*

Section III: Developing and Fighting for Purpose

Marva Renee Southall is a retired elementary and college level educator after 36 years. Writing is her hobby as well as her ministry. While teaching, she wrote and illustrated *I Can Do It: A Skills Activity Book for Home School Coordinators, Parents and Teachers* (Nashville Davidson County School, 1988). She is presently working on the revision of her first children's book. Marva and her brother, Kenneth, are members of Born Again Church in Nashville, Tennessee.

Eulogy of an Angel Reacher

Marva Southall

"You are very strong to be able to speak at your father's funeral," a church member said as I entered the foyer at Born Again church. It was not strength I wanted to share with others it was the miraculous events of what occurred during my Daddy's transition. I wanted them to know, beyond a shadow of a doubt, what I knew with my head, but now know with my heart.

There was not a coffin holding the shell of his remains in front of the well-wishers. Instead, the audience saw an array of oil paintings by my father, Walter Lee Southall. I walked to the podium wearing a modest black dress and a pearl necklace, but in my heart, I had on a dress filled with God's joy. It had an array of yellow, pink, and red

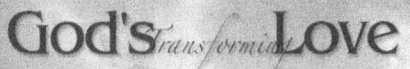

flowers against a sky blue background. The night before, I wondered how to tell them about Daddy. The church members only knew him as the man with the double prosthesis who I brought to church each Sunday in a wheelchair. However, once I started writing, the words flowed with ease.

"Silver and gold have I none; but such as I have give I thee" (Acts 3:6 KJV). That Scripture verse was what Peter said to the lame man before he was healed. What a perfect beginning! "Daddy did not have any money," I proclaimed, "but he left a wonderful legacy of tenacity, the gift of painting, and, most of all, a glimpse into what the future holds for believers."

I quickly gave an example of Daddy's tenacity. Not only did he continue working after he had his first leg amputated, but he also repaired the roof on his house. I told the audience how he taught himself to paint and that both of his children enjoyed art. They heard about his peaceful, content nature ninety eight percent of his life and how he used to say, "Nobody can pray better for Walter than Walter."

That "Walter praying" was the beginning of my adventure with him into what I call miraculous. I remember a time when Daddy (Walter) was in the ICU. He had diabetes, a stroke and arthritis had taken away his painting ability. The doctors had removed a bed sore, making an incision two inches by three inches on his bottom. Along with this constant pain, he could not breathe due to pneumonia, and he was on oxygen. His sweet, contented nature had changed to one of complaint, paranoia, and fear. One night, the staff in ICU allowed me to spend the night beside his bed.

Each breath was a strain as he began to wrestle with the fear of death. Between Daddy's labored breaths under the oxygen mask, he asked, "Am I going to hell?" I was surprised at his question because I have known of his love for the Lord all of my life. He showed it through his actions. Many of Daddy's paintings had Christian themes. His favorite was a large picture of Jesus on the cross with blood

Section III: Developing and Fighting for Purpose

streaming down His body, and a light shining on His blood puddled on the ground. My favorite painting was part of a series with candles representing different races of people and one transparent candle representing the Holy Spirit. There was another interesting oil painting in that series about the book of Revelation titled, "Old World, New Word."

Luckily, when he asked the question, I was able to quickly recite Romans 10:9–10 (NKJV), "If you confess with your mouth the Lord Jesus and believe in your heart that God has raised Him from the dead, you will be saved. For with the heart one believes unto righteousness, and with the mouth confession is made unto salvation."

He repeated parts of the scripture back to me and then said, "I believe, I believe! Is that enough?" I assured him that it was, but I do not think he thought that I knew what I was talking about. With each exhaled breath made, Daddy began to call out, "Jesus." This went on anytime he was awake that night: "Jesus," (breath); "Jesus," (breath); "Jesus" . . .

I needed to leave the hospital the next morning for a few hours. When I returned to ICU, he was not in his room. I braced myself for what I did not want to hear as I asked about his whereabouts at the nurse's station. The nurse on duty smiled and then gave me his room number. "*Wow*," I thought, "*After a night like that he is out of ICU.*" When I got to his room I was in for another surprise. The oxygen mask was gone, and Daddy was lying in bed smiling. Look at what calling on the name of Jesus did! During our talk, he told me that Elder Brown from our church came by and confirmed what I had said about being saved. I guess that was why he was smiling; Daddy's fears and doubts about his salvation had been confirmed by a trustworthy man of God.

Daddy must have asked Jesus to let him breathe without the oxygen mask because he only needed it for short intervals each day for the rest of his life. I wished he would have also asked God for the release of pain in his body. Just like when my mother transitioned from earth 11 years ago, the Holy Spirit had told me months before Daddy's

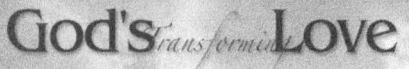

stroke that he would be leaving soon. So I was not in shock about the things that had happened to him, but I was very hurt over his suffering. The pain in his bottom must have been horrible. As long as the morphine was in his system, Daddy was fine, but it would wear off before his next scheduled dose. That was when the screams and moans began. Two nurses were required to move him or deal with personal needs because he was unable to move parts of his back. It was almost unbearable to see him in such misery. One night I decided to ask the doctor if Daddy could be on hospice care where the emphasis was on comfort. To my surprise that is exactly what she wanted to talk to me about. So we both agreed hospice was his best alternative.

His room at Alive Hospice on Patterson Street looked like the inside of a hotel with a hospital bed. There was a spacious bathroom, a high-gloss wooden wardrobe closet, a small table and chair, a recliner next to the bed, as well as a loveseat. Across from the bed was a television and a large window, which let the beauty of the courtyard show between the blinds.

Soft music played in the quiet halls that were lined with real flowers and beautiful paintings. I was thankful for the peace and homey surroundings. At first, Daddy was full of pain medicine, so he was able to talk, look at the TV, and was in much better spirits. After a while, he wanted me to feed him, then he would not eat at all, so food was no longer brought to him. I was assured that this was a normal part of the transition process. The effects of the morphine seemed to decrease. He moved from morphine injections to a series of stronger pain killers until he was using morphine, a pain killer patch, and a pain killer pump.

I do not remember the exact time, but after two or three weeks without eating anything, Daddy started doing what the chaplain called "angel reaching." While lying on his back, with his eyes fixed on the window, he slowly raised both arms at the same time, until they were at a 90-degree angle from his head. His arms would stay in that position for one to two minutes. Then he would slowly lower them, keeping them down for a few seconds, before he raised them again.

Section III: Developing and Fighting for Purpose

He would do this continuously for five to ten minutes at a time, speechless, with a constant determined gaze fixed upon the window. I tried to mimic his actions, but my arms got very tired long before he put his down. Also, it was hard to lower them slowly after being up for so long. I looked intently at the window and did not see anything different. The longest "angel reaching" happened between two and four each morning. He did it for shorter intervals of time during the day. I was full of questions. Why was he doing this? How did he get the energy to keep his arms up so long? Why didn't he quickly drop them back down when his arms became tired? What was he looking at? The chaplain told me some of their patient's "angel reached" before their transition. They were the ones who seemed to have a strong relationship with the Lord.

Then it happened! Usually, when he was in pain, waiting for the medicine in the pump to get into his blood stream, I would calm him by holding his hand and singing a song by Kurt Carr: "Something Happens." I was holding his hand and singing around three a.m.—a few days before his transition—when suddenly, with a great deal of force, Daddy jerked his hand from my embrace and started angel reaching. At first I felt rejected. Had he had enough of my singing? Did he want me to move from his bedside? Then I looked at his face. His eyes had that same determined glare at the window, but his expression is what gave me an insight into what may have been going on in the spiritual realm. Daddy's mouth was partly open with a smile. He was no longer moaning in pain. In fact, he looked joyful. I wondered if this was the expression the apostle Steven had in the book of Acts, when he was being stoned but was gazing into the heavens, seeing the Lord Jesus. I looked toward the window that held my father's attention. The blinds were closed. It was dark. I saw nothing.

What did he see that made him happy enough to forget his pain? Was it Jesus, angels, or maybe his mother, or wife who had been deceased for a number of years? Was it peace and beauty, or was it something too wonderful for me to comprehend? Whatever it was, Daddy wanted to be there.

Now, in my heart, I know that there is something fantastic waiting for believers on the other side of life when we are God's children. I rejoice that my father is in that wonderful place, and I take pleasure in telling others.

I ended his eulogy with a segment from the poem, "Go down Death" by James Weldon Johnson, which now has new meaning for me: "Weep not, weep not, [He] is not dead; [He's] resting in the bosom of Jesus."

Section III: Developing and Fighting for Purpose

Personal Life Reflection

Lilly Lester

1. Journaling: Who Am I? Why am I here?

2. On a scale of 1-10, how would rate your satisfaction with your life right now?

3. What is my life's purpose for this season?

4. Mediate on Micah 6:8. (NKJV)

5. Am I living according to God's deepest purpose for my life? If not, why?

Section III: Developing and Fighting for Purpose

EPILOGUE

GOD'S TRANSFORMING LOVE

Faith, Restoration, and Purpose

God is love. Embrace Him. Live in Him. God's love is transforming. This is the resounding echo of the stories written in this book. Read these true stories written by eighteen women, young and seasoned, who dared to share their journey. They are confronted with issues such as, depression, rejection, anger, forgiveness, shame, despair, hopelessness, grief, food addiction, self-identity, divorce, alcohol, and drug addiction. These over-comers tell it all, unashamedly to empower others in this journey called life.

God's Transforming Love is a must read! It is a refreshing, seemingly, face to face encounter with women who wear the Victor's Crown. There are treasured gems in these pages that will encourage you through the vicissitudes of life. Life's challenges and pains know no color, no age, no gender, and no financial status. You will be found somewhere in between the pages of this book. Brace yourself to experience the transforming love of God through your sighs, tears, joy, laughter, shock, and surprise, as you personally look within and reflect on faith, restoration, and purpose.

These eighteen women asked the same questions you have asked: How can I keep my family together? How can I face separation?

How can I keep my faith strong? God, I thought I trusted you? Why me Lord? What is my purpose? How can I face these giants? Lord, what did I do wrong? Why do I have to be so strong all the time? Read the book. It tells the story!

There are threads of faith, restoration and purpose resonating throughout the entire book. You will want to read this book and then purchase one for someone else. Then, you will be blessed the more, because you chose to share God's transforming love. Others can then walk toward wholeness, tell their story and share the book as well.

Peggy P. Enochs, Ed.D

Retired Administrator, Educator and Counselor

Section III: Developing and Fighting for Purpose

Contributors

Raquel Gammon has always been writing something (poetry, short stories, the next great novel) and is excited to begin sharing her stories with the world. For as long as she can remember, she has always had an idea in her head about a great story, and now has the opportunity to bring those stories to life. Raquel feels very blessed to be surrounded by women who share her same passion for writing. She has been working for over a year, assisting with several writing projects. She is currently working on her own projects, women's inspirational books. Raquel holds a B.A. in Psychology as well as a MBA and currently works in the healthcare industry. She lives in Nashville, TN and is a member of Olive Branch Church.

Gwendolyn E. Google is a retired, exceptional education teacher of 30-plus years. She feels that teaching is her life-long calling and passion, as she has ministered to young people of all ages, at school through the Fellowship of Christian Athletes and at home during meals around the kitchen table. "Mama Google," as she is affectionately known, continues to enjoy these relationships that God has put together over the years. Gwen looks forward to spending special times with her four adult children: Brice, Raymond, Regina, and Reggie Jr., who have been a great encouragement and support of her writing. Being a grandmother is an exciting part of Gwen's life, and she enjoys times with her nine grandchildren who know her as G-Ma. Gwen also feels blessed to have her mother, Jean Mackey, enjoying this season of her life with

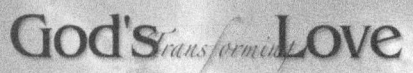

her, having mother-daughter, talks, shopping, and bonding. Gwen plans to take some pleasurable trips to other countries beginning with the Holy Land. Gwen also plans to continue writing books to encourage and help families and to write children's literature books.

Regina Conley-Hockett is a native of Nashville, Tennessee. She is the wife of Charles Lee Hockett and has one son, Dejuan Eugene Conley. She is the daughter of the late Elder Fred Conley and Willodes Conley Thompson. Regina is well known in Nashville, Tennessee, for her testimony of forgiveness after the tragic death of her twelve-year-old daughter, Adriane Dickerson. Regina is also president and CEO of Victorious Mothers of Murder, a support group that was birthed after her daughter's death. Regina has been providing support groups, retreats, and one-on-one counseling to families throughout the Nashville area. Victorious Mothers of Murder has several mothers who have joined Regina in her effort to reach families nationwide.

The mission of Victorious Mothers of Murder is to counsel, encourage, and provide a support system to share how we can be overcomers and victorious when we go through the process of grief after a violent loss. Regina says, "Violence affects families and communities in a very tragic way." She believes if we start early with violence prevention services, families will not have to experience the emotional stress that violent behaviors puts on families and communities.

She is a member of Born Again Church Christian Outreach Ministries, where her pastors are Bishop Horace and Kiwanis Hockett.

Wanda Hodge lives in Nashville Tennessee. Wanda lives and breathes to testify of God's grace and mercy toward her. Recently retired, she loves grand mothering her two grandchildren, singing in the choir, studying the word, cooking and extending a helping hand to those in need. From statistic to significance is the story of Wand's life. She now uses her faith and life experience to encourage, inspire and to bring to healing to others. Wanda is a woman of all seasons, in which she discovered to be Seasons of God and His Transforming love.

Section III: Developing and Fighting for Purpose

Ariel Jones is an alumnus of Lipscomb University with a B.A. in Journalism and New Media. She enjoys the simple things in life: God, family, friends, a good book or comic book, singing, humor, poetry and other hobbies. She is a published poetess and is currently working on a book of poetry that will be published in the near future. Ariel is also an aspiring actress and has been involved in several church plays and had the opportunity to perform at TPAC (Tennessee Performing Arts Center). She wouldn't be able to do anything without a great support system at home which includes a mother, father, and a younger brother. Her father, who transitioned to be with the Lord, pushed Ariel to be her best self and desired for her to whole heartedly seek the Lord as one who searches for water in a dry place. It is Ariel's prayer to be in line with God's Word and to have a heart for His people.

Joy Lester Perez is the proud mother of three beautiful adult children and the wife of Hector Perez. Writing, traveling and cooking are her hobbies. She co-authored "Expressions of His Glory" with scribe Lilly Lester; who is her mother. She is currently working on her first solo book entitled "Forgiven, Flawless and Free." She is a member of Faith, Hope and Love Fellowship. Her long term goals are to visit and do mission trips in countries such as Haiti and Africa.

Lilly Lester is a retired Educator and founder of Love Joy Collections and Creative Hands Writing Group. She has been an advocate for women and children for over 30 years. Her passions include spending time with her family, writing, and women's ministry. Lilly has authored four inspirational books and co-authored three others. Her writings and teachings have coached women to ignite and fan the flame into their kingdom purpose and to embrace change with anticipation and gratitude. Lilly is a retreat leader, teacher, speaker, and spiritual mother that inspires and impacts women from all walks of life. Lilly is actively involved in women's ministry at her home church, Born Again, in Nashville, Tenn. Lilly resides in Nashville, Tennessee with her husband of 49 years. They have two adult children, five grandchildren, and many spiritual sons and daughters

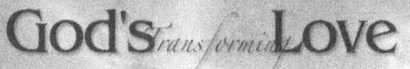

Sonya Little-Jones is a wife, mother, grandmother, and great-grandmother. She serves as a deaconess and secretary of Unity Baptist Church where the pastor is Rev. Harold O. Fields. Her most important role is that of being a daughter to the Master. She proclaims, "He has restored, reshaped, and renewed me." Often, God reminds her of His unending love toward her. She asks, "Who would have thought He would love me enough to give me another chance?" She and her husband reside in Salt Lake City, Utah.

Patricia Kluttz a native Bostonian, currently resides in Nashville, Tennessee, with her four children and six grandchildren. Patricia is a founding teacher in Nashville's first public Montessori school. She attends Born Again Church, where she enjoys being a part of the backstage crew in their Living Parables Ministry. Contrary to popular belief, working out takes a backseat to family and friends. She loves to laugh and hang out with her children. She loves music, the outdoors, and teaching and working with children. Patricia desires to one day go back to school and earn her doctorate in literacy. Patricia published her first book—a children's alphabet book—when at part of the nation of Islam, she and is working toward publishing two more children's books. She loves life and God!

Crystal Martin grew up in Cerritos, California. She decided to stay in the south after graduating from Western Kentucky University. She is a faithful member of Born Again Church and Christian Outreach Ministries in Nashville, TN. Crystal is the director for an organization that manages the aging. She presently resides in Smyrna, Tennessee. She has a son, and daughter. She loves to travel, and help people get true freedom in their finances.

Elder Karynthia A. G. Phillips is an author and ordained minister of the Gospel. Karynthia is bi-vocational as a minister and family practitioner. She is the Founder of Trinity Wholeness Ministries and works as a writers' coach for Spirit Lead Writers Network, which is based in Nashville, Tennessee. She is a freelance writer and speaker with three books to her credit. She has a passion for discipling others into spiritual maturity by the application of quiet

Section III: Developing and Fighting for Purpose

time. It is her hope that her works will enlighten and clarify the position of authority and power available to Christians, as God's principles in Scripture are implemented each day.

Her desire is to see Christians pursue a life of wholeness through understanding the fullness of the gift of salvation. Her mantra: The unity of body, spirit, and soul are essential to fulfill the purpose of God for your life. She believes that balance via self-care is obtained as one develops a personal relationship with God through private worship, during quiet time and practicing a healthy lifestyle. She is a wife of 33 years, the mother of 3 adult children, and a grandmother to 2 granddaughters.

Courtney Nicole Salters was born and raised in Tupelo, Mississippi and began her relationship with God at her home church, Kimble Chapel Missionary Baptist (KCMB) church. Her parents and grandparents were great examples of God's love and faithfulness and inspired her to develop her own relationship with God. Her understanding of God's character and attributes truly began to flourish in her college years, and her relationship with Him continues to grow.

His life through her has afforded great opportunities and blessings including, but not limited to the following: a beautiful family that loves her unconditionally, a Bachelor of Arts degree from Vanderbilt University (VU), a Master's in Business Administration from Belmont University, a great job working with students at VU, a loving church family at Born Again Church (BAC) in Nashville, TN, and a caring and fun group of friends who are also her prayer partners. She is eternally grateful to God for the great things He has done in her life.

Courtney is excited for the opportunity to share His great love in any way that she can, whether through prayer, singing in worship, counseling, ministering as an Elder at BAC, or writing her story in this book. This God given assignment marks the beginning of her journey as a writer, and she hopes to complete a book that expounds on the subject of food addiction and the abundance of His love and grace.

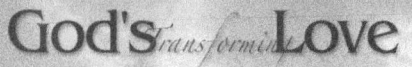

Rev. Lalita R. Smith, is a prophetic journalist, songwriter, poet, author, editor, minister, and Christian publishing consultant, who has been writing by inspiration for more than 35 years. She has dedicated the past three decades to offering assistance to various Christian writers who have been seeking guidance, leadership, and editorial assistance. She assists in bringing their God-inspired works to the marketplace. After relocating to Nashville from Southern California, she became a member of the Spirit Lead Writers Network while a member of Born Again Church.

She is an active member at Gateway Church in Southlake, Texas, under the leadership of Pastors Robert and Debbie Morris and is a regular participant at Glory of Zion with Dr. Chuck Pierce, in Corinth, Texas. For more information and to purchase her available products please visit: http://www.havilahhouse.weebly.com and http://www.patreon.com/Lalita

Elder Lucille Henderson Smith was born and raised in Minden, Louisiana. After completion of high school, she relocated to Los Angeles, California and attended South Western College. Later she pursued a career at the Veteran Administration Hospital, where she was an outstanding employee until she retired almost 31 years later. Early in life, Elder Smith recognized the call of God and began to teach and preach His word. After extensive Bible training, Elder Smith was ordained on October 4th, 2006 in Bluff Arkansas. She is an anointed speaker, teacher, and playwright. Elder Smith is one of God's ambassadors for a time such as this.

Elder Smith presently resides in Memphis, Tennessee. She is fulfilling her passion to "love people to life" and "letting her light shine before men". She has two daughters, one son, seven grandchildren and four great grandchildren.

Tonia Scott was born and raised in Nashville, Tennessee. She is currently working as an information technology security account administrator. She is also a licensed cosmetologist and as an independent consultant. She served on the Nashville State Community College Board and was a director of a Christian school's after-school care program.

She enjoys spending time with her family and being a wife and moth-

Section III: Developing and Fighting for Purpose

er. She rises early to prepare her home to be a home of peace and prayer. One of her favorite Scripture verses is from Proverbs 3:5–7: "Trust in the Lord with all your heart, And lean not on your own understanding; In all your ways acknowledge Him, And He shall direct your paths" (NKJV). Her hobbies are cooking, hosting guest in her home, scrapbooking, sewing, skating and helping others. She is an advocate for youth and children. Her *life speaks* as a motivational speaker.

Denotra Sharpe Sneed is a dedicated K-4th grade teacher at the Bethlehem Center of Nashville. Music is an integral part Denotra's life. She is known for sharing her gift throughout the body of Christ and with other Christian artists. She is a Praise and Worship Leader at Born Again Church in Nashville, Tennessee, ushering people in with the presence of God. Her forthcoming single, *Denotra,* is soon to be released. Denotra's ministry of praise and worship brings healing and revives the soul and spirit. Denotra lives in Nashville, Tennessee and is married to Charles Sneed.

Contact Information: charlesanddenotra@gmail.com or charlessneed@gmail.com

Marva Renee Southall is a retired elementary and college level educator after 36 years. Writing is her hobby as well as her ministry. While teaching, she wrote and illustrated *I Can Do It: A Skills Activity Book for Home School Coordinators, Parents and Teachers* (Nashville Davidson County School, 1988). She is presently working on the revision of her first children's book. Marva and her brother, Kenneth, are members of Born Again Church in Nashville, Tennessee.

Dr. Karen Wilkerson is an exceptional teacher, speaker and facilitator. She consults regularly with non-profits creating and streamlining systems. This "administrator extraordinaire" is known for her organizational skills, engaging workshops, seminars, and retreats. She inspires, encourages, mentors and empowers others to achieve their goals and dreams.

Wilkerson earned her Ed. D. in Administration specializing in Organization Development from Kennedy-Western University. She earned a M.S. in Marriage and Family Counseling from the University of Southern

Mississippi and a B.A. in Criminal Justice from the University of Southern Mississippi. She is currently working on her Ph. D. in Clinical Pastoral Counseling from Heritage Bible College and Seminary.

Karen sits and has sat on several boards including Gateway Institute, Safe Haven Family Shelter, The Christian Education Advisory Board, and Youth for Christ. She was an active member of Tennessee Business and Professional Women and was Region II District IV Director of the Tennessee Federation 2007-2008 BPW Leadership Team. Karen was voted as Administrator of the year in 2004 and 2005 among the Who's Who of Executives.

Karen is the mother of three wonderful children and lives with her husband of 29 years in Hendersonville, Tennessee.

www.ingramcontent.com/pod-product-compliance
Lightning Source LLC
Chambersburg PA
CBHW070109120526
44588CB00032B/1392